IMAGES OF

BATTLESHIPS:
THE FIRST BIG GUNS

RARE PHOTOGRAPHS FROM WARTIME ARCHIVES

PHILIP KAPLAN

Pen & Sword
MARITIME

First printed in Great Britain in 2014 by
Pen & Sword Maritime
an imprint of
Pen & Sword Books Ltd.
47 Church Street
Barnsley,
South Yorkshire
S70 2AS

A CIP record for this book is available from the British Library.

ISBN 978 1 78 346 2933

Printed and bound in England
By CPI Group (UK) Ltd. Croydon, CR0 4YY

Pen & Sword Books Ltd incorporates the Imprints of Pen & Sword Aviation, Pen & Sword Family History, Pen & Sword Maritime, Pen & Sword Military, Pen & Sword Discovery, Wharncliffe Local History, Wharncliffe True Crime, Wharncliffe Transport, Pen & Sword Select, Pen & Sword Military Classics, Leo Cooper, The Praetorian Press, Remember When, Seaforth Publishing and Frontline Publishing.

For a complete list of Pen & Sword titles please contact Pen & Sword Books Limited
47 Church Street, Barnsley, South Yorkshire, S70 2AS, England

E-mail: enquiries@pen-and-sword.co.uk
Website: www.pen-and-sword.co.uk

Contents

Reasonable efforts have been made to trace the copyright holders of all material used in this book. The author apologizes for any omissions. All reasonable efforts will be made in future editions to correct any such omissions. The author is grateful to the following people for the use of their published and/or unpublished mate-rial, and for their kind assistance in the preparation of this book: Charles Addis, Tony Alessandro, Robert Bailey, Malcolm Bates, Quentin Bland, Tony Briscomb, Charles Brown, Phoebe Clapham, Jack Delaney, Keith De Mello, Roger Ebert, Herb Fahr, Gary Fisher, Michael Fiske, Ella Freire, Oz Freire, Joseph Gilby, HMS Drake Photo Section, Mike Holloman, Eric Holloway, Tony Iacono, Jan Jacobs, Albert Lee Kaiss, Hargi Kaplan, Margaret Kaplan, Neal Kaplan, John Keegan, Richard Landgraff, Henry Leach, Maynard Loy, Eric Marsden, Ted Mason, Judy and Rick McCutcheon, Richard McCutcheon, Rita McCutcheon, James McMaster, Matilda McMaster, David Mellor, Richard Minear, Robert Oelrich, Ted Pederson, Harold Porter, Robert Sambataro, John Shelton, Christy Sheaff, Doug Siegfried, Mike Sizeland, Robert Shultz, Ian Smith, Mark Stanhope, Mark Thistlethwaite, Andrew Toppan. Please see page 144 for addition-al acknowlegments.

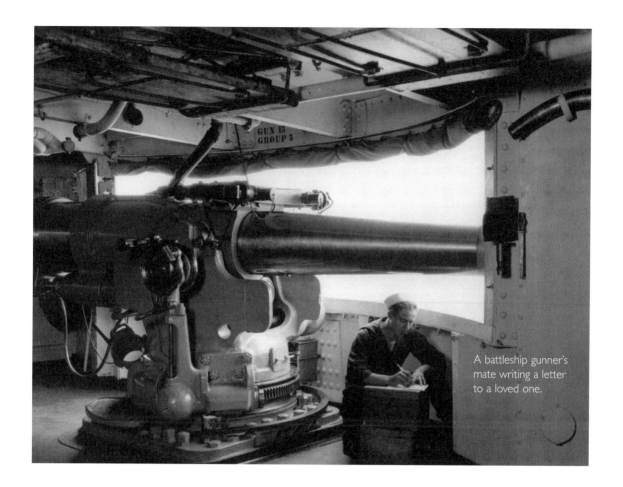

A battleship gunner's mate writing a letter to a loved one.

The First Battleships

Battles have been fought at sea for thousands of years, but naval warfare entered a new era in the late fifteenth century, when cannon became the principal armament of warships. From this period until the second half of the nineteenth century, when steam supplanted sail in the world's navies, naval tactics were dominated by the 'line of battle'. This formation, consisting of a line of ships sailing, parallel with or at an angle to a similar line of opposing ships, enabled the rows of guns along the ship's side to bring maximum firepower to bear on the enemy. A ship that was big and powerful enough to take its place in the line of battle was called a 'ship of the line' or a 'battleship'.

Ships of the line might vary significantly in size and armament—in Lord Nelson's navy they might carry anything between seventy-four and 120 guns—but they were all signficantly superior to frigates, sloops, brigs and the other lesser craft; they were all what navies later came to call 'capital ships.'

Preserved in the historic Naval Dockyard at Portsmouth, England, are three examples of 'capital ships', one from the beginning of the age of 'classical' naval warfare, one from its zenith and the third from the point when steam began to eclipse sail. The Tudor *Mary Rose*, the oldest of these, was commissioned in 1509 by King Henry VIII, as the first real warship of the young Royal Navy. Named after the King's favourite sister, *Mary Rose* was launched at Portsmouth in 1511 and became the flagship of the Royal Navy. She was 127 feet long at her waterline, with a beam of thirty-eight feet and a draught of fifteen feet. Her ultimate displacement, after being refitted, was 727 tons.

Mary Rose was constructed of oak and elm and armed with muzzle-loading guns made of cast bronze and breech-loading guns of wrought-iron. In order to ensure that her guns were made to the highest standard of the day, the king imported the finest gun-founders from France. Her armament also included a large number of skilled bowmen whose task was to kill the crewmen of enemy vessels. She was normally manned by a crew of between 300 and 400.

Unlike most fighting ships of the time, the *Mary Rose* was designed specifically as a warship. Mindful of her role as a defence against England's potential enemies, which included France and Scotland, the king himself specified how she was to be equipped; the result was an innovative vessel which can legitimately be described as a prototypical battleship. Rather than having her guns mounted mainly on the 'castles' at either end of the hull like her predecessors, her designers pioneered the use of big guns down a row each side of the hull near the waterline, enabling her to fire broadside barrages at enemy vessels. In another break from tradition, her planking was positioned edge to edge, in a Carvel-type construction, rather than being overlapped. This technique made for a much more watertight hull.

In 1512 the *Mary Rose* took part in her first battle. In September of the previous year the Pope and the King of Aragon had entered into an alliance against Louis XII of France. In January 1512, the English Parliament voted to ally the country with Spain and preparations were made for *Mary Rose* to sail as flagship of Admiral Sir Edward Howard. On 10 August that year she led twenty-five other warships in an attack on the French fleet at Brest, which Admiral Howard estimated at 222 ships. He immediately attacked the French flagship, the 790-ton *Grande Louise*. At the end of the two-day raid, Howard returned to Portsmouth in triumph, having captured thirty two French vessels and 800 seamen.

Mary Rose campaigned effectively for the king through the subsequent years during which Henry devoted much money and effort to fortifying his coastal approaches against attack by the French. At Portsmouth an enormous chain boom extending to the Gosport shore, to seal off the harbour entrance was installed. In a two-month campaign against France in 1544, English forces captured the port of Boulogne, tightening their control over the Channel. By spring of 1545, however, Henry faced the prospect of a major French attack on Portsmouth, his principal naval base on the south coast, which was intended to destroy Henry's warships and other vessels in their anchorage, and to sever English supply lines to Boulogne. On 18 July, the French fleet anchored in St Helen's Roads near the Isle of Wight. As the commander-in-chief of his forces, the king waited at Portsmouth for the threatened French landings. His fortifications there included the Square and Round Towers which oversaw the deepwater channel, and the gun batteries of Southsea Castle. Treacherous shallows near the harbour posed an additional hazard to the enemy ships.

The French had assembled a fleet of 225 ships with 30,000 men, while Henry faced them with just 100 ships and 12,000 men. He met with his naval commanders and then went ashore to watch his fleet sail out to meet the enemy. His ships turned south out of Portsmouth harbour, between Spit Sand and Horse Sands; but although there were some clashes between

above: The *Mary Rose*, pride of the English Fleet

the two sides that day, little resulted from the early exchanges of cannon fire before night fell.

The following day the sea was calm and the French galleys advanced on the English warships, attempting to draw them out into open battle. Then suddenly the *Mary Rose* heeled over and sank. A French account claims that she was hit by French cannon. English accounts differ considerably, though they suggest that, while hoisting sail and preparing to get under way, *Mary Rose* suddenly heeled as she came about. Her gunports were open, with her cannon run out ready for action and as she heeled, seawater rushed over the gunport sills, destabilizing the vessel and causing her to capsize and quickly sink.

The *Mary Rose* was the main casualty of what turned out to be little more than an inconclusive skirmish.

Attempts to raise her failed, and it was only in 1982 that she was lifted from the seabed and taken to the dockyard where she had been built.

In the two centuries that followed the sinking of the *Mary Rose*, Britain, along with France, the Netherlands, Portugal and Spain, developed a large colonial empire, and a powerful naval fleet to oppose any threat to their freedom of the seas. Britain had the advantage numerically, but France and other nations were more advanced in the design and construction of warships that were larger, faster, and more stable. However, the superior quality of the British crews and officers who excelled in their training, gunnery skills, and discipline resulted in the dominance of the British fleet until the American War of Independence. In that conflict the French sided with the Americans against Britain, and Spain allied herself with France, posing

top left: An English stone cannonball; right: The *Duke of Wellington* in 1855, flagship of the British Royal Navy's Baltic Fleet; below: French Admiral Pierre Suffren.

a combined invasion threat which the British had to take most seriously. Within a decade of the end of the American war, that threat became more substantial as Napoleon Bonaparte began his adventures across Europe. In 1783, the British were defeated by the Americans and the Royal Navy was no longer the feared force it had been for nearly three hundred years.

The most famous warship in British history is HMS *Victory*, the flagship of the Royal Navy fleet at Trafalgar. Crewed by 850 men, *Victory* was 226 feet long with a beam of fifty-two feet and a draught of twenty-one feet. She was built of oak, elm, fur, and pine and her hull was sheathed in copper. Her armament was 102 cast-iron cannon ranging from twelve to thirty-two-pounders, along with two sixty-eight-pounders. She spent the first years of the nineteenth century sailing at the head of the British fleet in the Meditarranean and Atlantic oceans for several years, trying to draw the French fleet into battle. Then, in October 1805, Admiral Villeneuve, in command of the French fleet, took his warships out of port at Toulon to join with the Spanish fleet at Cadiz. Napoleon had abandoned whatever plans he may have had for invading England, and his combined naval force was proceeding to Naples where they were to operate in support of troops against Italy.

Heading into what would be one of the last great open-sea battles of the age of sail, in the early hours of 29 October, Nelson's force awaited that of Villeneuve and the Spanish commander, Rear Admiral Charles-René Magon, in the Straits of Gibraltar at Cape Trafalgar.

above: The French warship *Gloire* in 1860; right: The American
Navy's turreted *Monitor* in battle with the CSS *Virginia* (formerly the
Merrimac) during the 1861-1865 Civil War.

Contrary to strict Admiralty policy, Nelson chose to attack the French and Spanish warships using a new tactic he had devised. He would lead his ships in two separate parallel battle lines at a nearly 90 degree angle to the enemy line, causing their ships to scatter and providing his captains with the opportunity to engage their opponents in ship-to-ship actions. In fact, this approach put *Victory* and his other ships in greater danger than the conventional tactic would have done, but Nelson took the risk, in the belief that the French and Spanish gunners were poorly trained and unskilled and the British gunners at least three times faster at their work than was the enemy.

At 11 a.m., on 21 October, the crew of *Victory* made her guns ready for action. With little wind, the ships of Nelson's force were making just one and a half knots as they approached the French and Spanish vessels. It was nearly 11:30 a.m. when Nelson sent his "England expects" flag signal to his fleet, followed immediately by the signal "Engage the enemy more closely". At about this time, some of the enemy ships began firing at Nelson's warships, checking their ranges, which were already very short. As the distance continued to close, *Victory* was taking hits and losing crewmen. She manoeuvred to slide between the French flagship *Bucentaure* and another enemy vessel, the *Redoubtable*. While passing *Bucentaure* at a distance of less than forty feet, the gunners of *Victory* launched a broadside blast at the French flagship, hitting it with a force sufficient to cause nearly 400 casualties. The broadside exchange continued and, by 4 p.m., the battle had ended in triumph for the British, and in tragedy as well. In the midst of the cannon fire, Admiral Nelson was mortally wounded by a French sniper. The battle re-established the Royal Navy as the dominant naval force

in the world. Napoleon would not be invading England, and the world had witnessed what a well-led, well-trained and disciplined fleet could achieve, even when faced with an enemy whose vessels were faster and better armed. As Ian Johnston and Rob McAuley stated in their book *The Battleships*: "If ever there was an example of a 'battleship' that became a symbol of national pride, it is surely HMS *Victory*—still in commission in the Royal Navy, beautifully preserved and restored, she is the ultimate example of the power and the majesty of a line-of-battle ship of 100 guns—an eighteenth century ancestor of the great battleships that were to follow."

After Trafalgar, the British fleet sailed wherever it chose to go, virtually unchallenged.

Both the British and French navies were mightily impressed by the effectiveness of the new shells fired from sixty-eight-pounder guns on the Russian line-of-battle ships during their bombardment of Turkish warships at Sinope in the Crimean War of 1853. These shells, replacing cannon balls, exploded on impact with their Turkish targets, stting them on fire. The French and British answer to this new threat was a type of floating gun platform covered in four-inch armour plate. These gun-battery platforms were powered by steam engines giving them a speed of four knots and were manoeuvred into firing position by tugs. This combination of radical advances in armour and armament technologies would lead to the development of the twentieth-century battleship. British domination of the seas extended into the later nineteenth century, when steam power and the industrial revolution made possible the first generation of metal-hulled vessels. The development of shells or projectiles capable of breaching the hulls of vulnerable wooden warships had led to ironclads. Warships could be built to previously impossible sizes, but iron hulls brought with them the need to devise new and different armament, along with shells or projectiles capable of breaching these strong new hulls.

The navies of the world were no longer dependent upon the wind and its direction. Steam power, and the new screw propeller enabled an entirely new form of vessel to come into being, and in 1860, an important new battleship was completed, the first of four vessels of the *Gloire* class of French battleships. Though still rigged for sail, her design featured engines developing 2,500 horsepower which drove a propeller shaft giving *Gloire* a top speed of thirteen knots. She had a crew of about 570 men. Her displacement was 5,630 tons. Her length was 255 feet at the waterline; her beam was fifty-six feet and her draught was twenty-eight feet. She was armed with thirty-six 6.4-inch muzzle-loading guns down both sides of her decks. She was protected by a 4.7-inch wrought-iron armour belt which extended down both sides of her hull to a depth of five feet.

The French intended to build up to thirty *Gloire* class battleships; they actually completed ten. Limited iron-making capacity in France meant that only *Couronne*, of the first four ships in the class, would have an iron hull.

With the completion of *Gloire*, building activity on an iron-clad warship for Britain was greatly increased. Two such vessels, *Warrior* and *Black Prince*, were under construction. They were modern, pioneering vessels whose technology would greatly influence future battle-

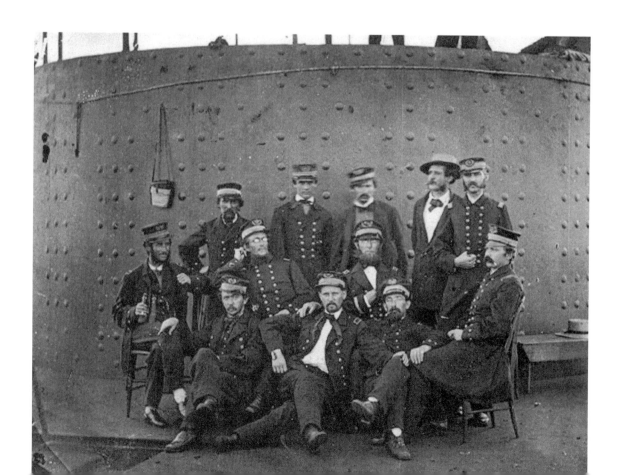

ships and whose appearance, in 1861 and 1862 respectively, ended the brief lead which France had gained in warship design with *Gloire*.

A purpose-built battleship, the 9,137-ton *Warrior* significantly raised the standard for warships. Much faster, better armed and armoured than *Gloire*, the iron-hulled *Warrior* was an innovative fighting vessel that incorporated advances such as forced ventilation on the gun-deck to get rid of smoke, a laundry with hand-operated washing machines, and a blast furnace in the boiler room to produce molten iron used in hollow shot. *Warrior* was 420 feet long with a beam of fifty-eight feet and a draught of twenty-six feet. She had a 4.5-inch armour belt and her armament consisted of ten 110-pounders, twenty-six sixty-eight-pounders, and four seventy-pounders. She carried a crew of 700 men. Like the *Victory*, *Warrior* has been lovingly restored and may be visited at the Naval Dockyard in Portsmouth.

In America, the Civil War of 1861-65 spurred the design and construction of what had been a European concept, the turret-gunned warship. To meet the challenge of the new CSS *Virginia* (formerly the steam frigate *Merrimac*), a low-set, floating battery armed with eight nine-inch guns set in armoured gun ports, and two seven-inch rifled shell-guns, the U.S. Navy commissioned the *Monitor*. Designed by inventor John Ericsson, *Monitor* was essentially a steam-powered raft which featured a rotating turret twenty feet in diameter housing two eleven-inch smooth-bore guns. After encountering and sinking two U.S. Navy frigates at Hampton Roads, near the entrance to Chesapeake Bay on 8 March 1862, *Virginia* was engaged the next day by *Monitor* in a three-hour battle. It ended inconclusively when both vessels

left and right: Views of the Union Navy gunboat *Monitor* , victorious in her battle action with the CSS *Virginia*.

left and below: HMS *Warrior*; right: American steamboats that plied the Mississippi late in the nineteenth century.

withdrew, each unable to penetrate the armour of their adversary. This clash of new and unconventional warship types established that their heavy armour seemed invulnerable to attack, and that a layout of fixed guns along the length of a battleship was no match for a vessel with turret-mounted guns able to fire in any direction. It was clear too, that the development of more powerful guns and shells would be crucial to overcoming the advances in armour plating that had been demonstrated by *Virginia* and *Monitor*. But, while these powerful new warships foreshadowed future developments, they had been designed solely for fighting in calm coastal water. Something quite different would be required for the new form

of combat to come on the open seas.

By the last years of the nineteenth century, dramatic increases in production allowed steel to replace iron in the construction of warships. By then, steam had almost entirely replaced sails as the power source for such vessels. It was a time in which great maritime nations like Britain, Germany, Japan, Russia and the United States set out to build powerful and impressive new navies centred around giant, blue-water battleships.

Borne each by other in a distant line, / the sea-built forts in dreadful order move; / So vast

the noise, as if not fleets did join / But lands unfixed, and floating nations strove. / Now passed on either side they nimbly tack; / Both strive to intercept and guide the wind; / And, in its eye, more closely they come back, / To finish all the deaths they left behind.
—from *Annus Mirabilis* by John Dryden

I am a great inventor, did you but know it. I have new weapons and explosives and devices to substitute for your obsolete tactics and tools. Mine are the battle-ships of righteousness and integrity—The armour plates of quiet conscience and self-respect—the impregnable conning tower of divine manhood—The Long Toms of persuasion—The machine-guns of influence and example—The dum-dum bullets of pity and remorse—The impervious cordon of sympathy—The concentration camps of brotherhood—the submarine craft of forgiveness—The torpedo boat-destroyer of love—And behind them all the dynamic of truth! I do not patent my inventions. Take them. They are free to all the world.
—from *War and Hell* by Ernest Crosby

Soldiers of the Union Army during the American
Civil War, 1861-1865.

Launched on 29 December 1860, HMS *Warrior* might well have been called Peacemaker, for in her entire career at sea she never fired a shot in anger. Her mere presence in several encounters brought a calming effect to what otherwise would have been hostilities.

Her crew consisted of forty-two officers, three warrant officers, 455 seamen and boys, thirty-three Royal Marine non-commissioned officers, 118 Royal Marine artillerymen, two chief engineers, ten engineers and sixty-six stokers and trimmers. She served in the British fleet for many years before being relegated to the Reserve Fleet. In 1883 she was withdrawn from service and her masts and guns were stripped from her. In 1924, *Warrior* was put up for sale and the buyer then used her as a floating oil jetty at Pembroke Dock in Wales.

A black viscious ugly customer as ever I saw, whale-like in size, and with as terrible a row of incisor teeth as ever closed on a French frigate.
—Charles Dickens on HMS *Warrior*

In the sixteenth century, before the advent of commercial fertilizer, great quantities of manure were transported by ship. It was stored in dry bundles, weighing far less in that form than when wet, and in dry form it was not subject to fermentation. When at sea, however, the manure occasionally became damp, causing the process of fermentation to begin. Methane gas is a by-product of this process, and the danger of its presence was soon discovered, probably by a seaman who brought a lighted lantern with him when he visited the cargo hold. Several ships were destroyed by mysterious explosions before the cause was discovered. Once the cause of these explosions was understood, shippers began stamping the bundles: SHIP HIGH IN TRANSIT, directing cargo handlers to store the bundles high enough in the ship to prevent water or damp from reaching the cargo.

Whoever commands the sea commands that trade; whosoever commands the trade of the world commands the riches of the world, and consequently the world itself.
—from *Historie of the World* by Sir Walter Raleigh, first published in 1614

top left: Commander of the Army of the Confederacy, General Robert E. Lee; right: Lee's Union Army counterpart, General Ulysses S. Grant, whose victory in the Civil War in 1865 led to his becoming the eighteenth president of the United States in March 1869; left: Casualties of the Civil War; right: The Confederate CSS *Virginia*.

Tsushima

When naval forces of Russia and Japan met in battle at 2 p.m. on 27 May 1905 off the island of Tsushima near the Straits of Korea, it was the first large engagement between big-gun warships. It was really a test of the warships and tactics of Britain versus those of France. Many of the Japanese ships involved were British-built, with mostly British weapons and equipment. The Russian vessels were largely based on French designs and engineering and the participating Russian shipyards were principally financed with French investment. The Japanese fleet at Tsushima included six battleships and nine armoured cruisers. Of these, all of the battleships and five of the cruisers were British-made.

In 1902 Britain and Japan had signed a formal alliance recognizing their common interest in preventing further expansionism by Russia. It was a mutual assistance pact whereby both nations would co-operate to help maintain the principle of free trade in Chinese waters, and a counter to the Russian threat to Korea, Manchuria and other countries in the region.

The war began when the Japanese navy conducted a surprise attack on the Russian Pacific Fleet at Port Arthur on mainland China on the night of 8/9 February 1904. Both Russia and Japan wanted control of the Far East seas, but the Russians had not imagined that the Japanese would go so far as war. In the raid, Japanese Imperial Navy Admiral Heihachiro Togo ordered five destroyers into the narrow harbour in a torpedo attack on the Russian fleet. Two of the seven Russian battleships sheltering in Port Arthur, *Tsarevitch* and *Retvizan*, as well as the cruiser *Pallada*, were hit, hampering the Russian fleet's capability long enough for Japanese forces to land in Korea virtually unopposed. These troops then advanced across the Yalu River to threaten the Russians at Port Arthur. The next day Togo, in his flagship the battleship *Mikasa*, led a force of sixteen warships in a bombardment of the vessels at Port Arthur. The Russian ships were blockaded in the port and some of the warships tried unsuccessfully to break the siege in an action on 25 February. Two Japanese battleships, *Yashima* and *Hatsue*, ran into Russian mines, exploded and sank.

As a young man, the Russian Tsar had been attacked by a lunatic while touring Japan and

Russian battleships at the Battle of Tsushima.

ever since then had nursed a profound hatred of the Japanese. In April 1904, he resolved to use his Baltic fleet to teach the Japanese a lesson they would never forget, and to restore Russian prestige at the same time. But by late August the situation for the Russians had deteriorated dramatically. With their Pacific fleet bottled up, they were vulnerable to sea attack from the east; an intolerable situation. They determined to use any means necessary to eliminate this threat from Japan, including the rash measure of deploying their Baltic fleet to the Far East.

Preparing to move the fleet halfway around the world was a logistical nightmare for Russian naval commander Admiral Zinovy Rozhdestvensky, who had been Russian Naval Attaché in London between 1892 and 1894 and was under no illusions about the capabilities of the British warship industry, especially in comparison to that of Russia. Russia had no

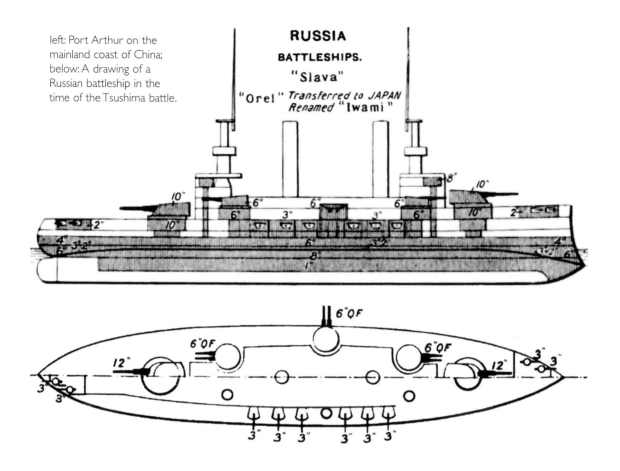

left: Port Arthur on the mainland coast of China; below: A drawing of a Russian battleship in the time of the Tsushima battle.

RUSSIA

BATTLESHIPS.

"Slava"

"Orel" *Transferred to JAPAN Renamed* "Iwami"

bases or port facilities of her own to serve the admiral's ships along his route, compelling him to transport all the coal and provisions which his vessels required, as well as medical and repair capabilities and everything else that his men and ships would need for the voyage and the epic battle to follow.

Rozhestvensky steamed out of Kronstadt in late September. While moving through the North Sea on the night of 22 October, the Russian vessels somehow became involved in a confusing and tragic action in which they fired on four British fishing trawlers, setting them on fire. Britain readied for war with Russia and sent out cruisers to stalk the Baltic warships as they passed down the Channel and on towards Spain. But tempers cooled as the Russian ships proceeded further south.

Admiral Rozhdestvensky split the Baltic fleet in two as it approached Tangier at the end of December. He sent the smaller vessels through the Suez Canal and took the big ships around the Cape of Good Hope. The difficulties he faced were considerably increased when, on 1 January 1905, a signal arrived informing him that the Japanese had taken Port Arthur. At the end of his extremely demanding journey he would no longer have the use of either the battleships of Russia's Pacific fleet or the Port Arthur facility. He would have to take his fleet on to the only other port open to him, Vladivostok, via the straits between Japan and Korea. The admiral informed the Tsar by telegram that the best he could do was to break

through to Vladivostok. The Tsar replied angrily that the admiral's mission was "to master the Sea of Japan". The pragmatic admiral felt little optimism about the fate his squadron would face when it encountered the Japanese fleet in its home waters.

On 27 May, the Russian fleet reached a position near the island of Tsushima. Awaiting it was Admiral Togo and his fleet, with four battleships, including Togo's flagship *Mikasa*, *Fuji*, *Asahi*, and *Shikishima* in the vanguard. They were accompanied by twenty cruisers of which ten were heavy, twenty-one destroyers and several smaller vessels. The 15,000-ton battleships were armed with four twelve-inch guns and fourteen six-inch guns each and could make eighteen knots. The Russian fleet had the advantage in numbers with eleven battleships, four of them new. They displaced 13,500 tons each and carried four twelve-inch guns and twelve six-inch guns. Their maximum speed was 17.5 knots. As he led his fleet into battle, Togo signalled them: "The fate of our Empire rests on this action. Let every man do his utmost."

The seas were high as the opposing fleets closed the distance between them in the early afternoon of the 27th. In the difficult conditions, the Russian admiral brought his fleet in at nine knots, while Admiral Togo elected to charge at top speed. At the precise moment, Togo's ships turned to cross the "T" of the Russian vessels, positioning the Japanese warships so that all of their big guns could be brought to bear on the Russians, who, for their part could only reply with their forward weapons.

Shortly after firing commenced, it was clear that the Japanese crews were serving their guns, sighting and firing with greater efficiency than their opponents. Massive fires soon raged through the big Russian ships *Alexander III*, *Osliabya*, and *Suvarov*, the flagship of Admiral Rozhdestvensky. The forward turret of *Osliabya* was destroyed and in half an hour further

both: Battle damage to
the Russian cruiser *Oleg*.

damage caused her to capsize and sink. A shell smashed into the bridge of *Suvarov*, serious-ly wounding Rozhdestvensky, who was evacuated to a destroyer soon afterwards when it was apparent that *Suvarov* could not be saved. By late afternoon, heavy smoke and mist were obscuring the battle area, reducing Togo's ability to target the Russian ships accurately. The conditions enabled the Russians to quickly regroup and withdraw towards Vladivostok. But the ships of the Japanese pursued the Russians and continued to pound them. Their heavi-est fire was directed at the battleships *Borodino* and *Alexander III*, both of which were sent to the bottom of the straits by early evening. Now Togo launched his destroyers in a torpedo attack which soon resulted in the sinking of the battleship *Sissoi Veliki* and the cruisers *Vladimir Monomakh* and *Admiral Makarov*. The one-sided battle continued into the following day, with the Japanese destroying most of what remained of the Russian fleet. When it was over, just three Russian vessels, a cruiser and two destroyers, all badly damaged, managed to limp into port at Vladivostok. The final score amounted to eleven Russian warships sunk, four captured and three interned in the Philippines. Japanese ship losses amounted to three torpedo boats. The Russians lost 5,045 sailors killed, with 6,106 taken prisoner. Japan lost 110 killed and suf-fered 590 wounded. The Russian fleet had been annihilated and Russia was no longer a world-class sea power. The Odessa mutiny of June 1905, during which the crew of the bat-tleship *Potemkin* shot their officers and took control of the ship, served to underline the weakness of the Russian political and naval establishment.

The Battle of Tsushima is seen by most historians as one of the most important and deci-sive engagements in naval history. It demonstrated the ship-killing power of the big gun at sea and confirmed the dangers posed by torpedoes. It produced in the Japanese a sense of pride in their achievement and a confidence that they were a significant naval power and

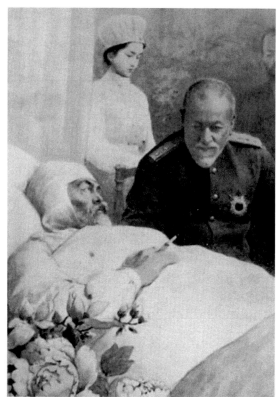

would continue to be one in the future.

The rest of the world was in awe of what the Japanese had achieved at Tsushima. Europe was shocked and surprised at the outcome, and alarmed at the prospect of a new and possibly more aggressive posture on the part of Japan throughout Asia as her influence there expanded. With her defeat of the Russian fleet, Japan came to believe in the importance of shedding her dependence on foreign sources for her warships and weaponry. She began intense efforts to develop steel mills and shipyards, mainly for battleship construction at Kure, Sasebo, and other ports. While her navy enjoyed its new command of the Far Eastern seas, Japan's armies in Manchuria were dominating that war front. With her ultimate victory she retained Port Arthur, the South Manchurian railway and an overarching position in Korea.

Observers at Tsushima attributed the Japanese victory to the better handling of their ships and to their highly disciplined adherence to sound naval doctrine and procedure. It is also fair to say that the quality of leadership in the Russian navy had declined greatly after the death of its key commander, Admiral Makarov, in the explosion of the battleship *Petro Pavlovsk* when it struck a Japanese mine near Port Arthur in April.

Perhaps most significantly, Tsushima served to point the way forward for naval tactics in the twentieth century. It demonstrated that fewer rounds, very well aimed and fired at a decisive range from the heavy guns of battleships, would yield far more effective results than many rounds delivered relatively quickly from lighter guns. The victorious Admiral Togo had proved a clever, formidable warrior, capitalizing on superior speed in his attacks at Tsushima, instilling in his crews efficiency, skill, determination, discipline and patience, all of which paid off handsomely in his overwhelming defeat of the Russian adversary. His prudent yet opportunistic management of his ships, and his facility in effectively employing both big gun and torpedo attacks, impressed the changing world.

There is a tide in the affairs of men, / Which, taken at the flood, leads on to fortune .
—from *Julius Caesar*, Act IV, Scene III by William Shakespeare

Men appear to prefer ruining one another's fortunes and cutting each other's throats about a few paltry villages, to extending the grand means of human happiness.
—Voltaire

Diplomats are just as essential to starting a war as soldiers are for finishing it. You take diplomacy out of war and the thing would fall flat in a week.
—Will Rogers

"*The Battleship Potemkin* has been famous for so long that it is almost impossible to come to it with a fresh eye. It is one of the fundamental landmarks of cinema. Its famous massacre on the Odessa Steps has been quoted so many times in other films (most notably in *The Untouchables*) that it's likely many viewers will have seen the parody before they see the original. The film once had such power that it was banned in many nations including its native Soviet Union. Governments actually believed it could incite audiences to action. If today it seems more like a technically brilliant but simplistic 'cartoon' (Pauline Kael's description in a favorable review), that may be because it has worn out its element of surprise—that, like the 23rd Psalm or Beethoven's Fifth, it has become so familiar we cannot percieve it for what it is.
　"The movie was ordered up by the Russian revolutionary leadership for the twentieth anniversary of the *Potemkin* uprising, which Lenin had hailed as the first proof that troops could be counted on to join the proletariat in overthrowing the old order.
　"As sketched by Eisenstein's film, the crew members of the battleship, cruising the Black Sea after returning from the war with Japan are mutinous because of poor rations. There is a famous close-up of their breakfast meat, crawling with maggots.
　After officers throw a tarpaulin over the rebellious ones and order them to be shot, a firebrand named Vakulinchuk cries out, 'Brothers! Who are you shooting at?' The firing squad lowers its guns, and when an officer unwisely tries to enforce his command, full-blown mutiny takes over the ship"
—Roger Ebert, film critic

far left: Russian Admiral Zonovy Rozhdestvensky; Admiral Heihachiro Togo visiting Rozhdestvensky in the Russian admiral's hospital room after the battle.

Dreadnought

The battleship HMS *Dreadnought* entered service with the British Royal Navy in 1906 and was such a great advance in naval technology that the name dreadnought was given to the generation of battleships that followed in her wake. Admiral Sir John A. 'Jacky' Fisher was known as the "father of the dreadnought". He established a design committee to research and evaluate battleship and warship design and construction ideas for the Royal Navy.

It was the rapid development of steam turbine engines for sea-going vessels, particularly the designs of Charles Parsons, that had impressed the Royal Navy's Committee on Designs in their planning sessions for *Dreadnought*. In that period a number of ships of various types and sizes were being fitted with turbines and undergoing sea trials. Cunard was preparing to fit them into its new passenger liners, *Mauretania* and *Lusitania*. Turbine power was clearly the wave of the future in warship design.

In the first years of the twentieth century naval planners realized that the torpedo could no longer be dismissed as a mere novelty but had to be respected as a genuine threat. Torpedoes were becoming reliable, accurate weapons of substantial range. The obvious counter was to deploy larger caliber naval guns which could strike the enemy from beyond torpedo range. The lessons of the Battle of Tsushima served to reinforce this new philosophy. In May 1905, the same month as Tsushima, the British First Sea Lord, Vice-Admiral Sir John 'Jacky' Fisher, put Britain in the forefront of a battleship revolution when he authorized construction of the first of an entirely new class of capital ships, the first 'all big-gun' battleship, HMS *Dreadnought*.

Fisher was no expert in the fields of warship design or naval gunnery, but he was determined that the Royal Navy would be modernized and prepared to meet the growing challenge posed by the German fleet. His own challenge was to provide the navy with a new warship of great capability, but at relatively low cost. The British treasury would not stand for what might be perceived as an extravagance that would anger the taxpayers. *Dreadnought* would be expensive, so Fisher called for a substantial reduction in the British warship inventory and the scrapping of hundreds of ships which he claimed were "too weak to fight and too slow to run away". He also included cruisers in his list of eliminations, as he believed that the Royal Navy's future lay with a proliferation of submarines, destroyers and fast battleships. His cuts brought impressive economies along with a leaner and meaner fleet.

The most important single feature of *Dreadnought*, as compared with her predecessors, was the use of steam turbine power. This, and her further assets of heavy, long-range gun

left: Admiral Sir John Fisher, First Sea Lord of the Board of Admiralty; far left: A bow view of the American superdreadnought USS *Arizona*.

below: The big guns of *Dreadnought*;
bottom: A rear view of the pioneering
battleship.

armament and improved armour, perfectly suited Fisher's main interest—to show the world, and especially Germany, France, Russia, and the United States, that Britain still ruled the waves and would continue to do so.

Fisher believed in the value of a deterrent. Never one to shy from publicity, he decided to produce *Dreadnought* in a single year and to use the project as a means of impressing the world with Britain's naval invincibility, shipbuilding strength and industrial capacity. He was set on Britain being first to launch, conduct trials and operate the new class of battleship and was utterly ruthless in his pursuit of that aim.

His zeal for the project was most evident when a major delay was encountered in production of the gun turrets for the new vessel. To circumvent the problem, Fisher ordered a number of shortcuts; in particular, he had turrets, mountings, and armour plates, which had been intended for two other battleships, *Lord Nelson* and *Agamemnon*, diverted for installation in *Dreadnought*. The 1,100 workers of the Portsmouth Shipyard laid down *Dreadnought* in October 1905 and by February 1906 the new ship had been launched. On 3 October, in a record-breaking building time, she was readied for preliminary trials. From the laying of her keel to completion, *Dreadnought*'s construction took just 366 days. In fact, her final fitting-out took an additional two months, but her coming-out party made all other capital ships in the world obsolete. Henceforth, battleships fell into two groups: the pre-dreadnoughts and dreadnoughts—the word is still used as a generic for even the last generation of battleships.

Dreadnought was larger than any previous battleship. She looked, and was, formidable and revolutionary. With long, clean lines, and huge turrets spaced along her deck, she was a superb gun platform. Her performance during sea trials was gratifying; her gunnery judged excellent with two aimed rounds a minute fired per piece. Her structure was fully up to the stress of firing eight-gun broadsides. Powered by steam-driven quadruple-screw turbines, she was capable of 21.6 knots and had a range of 6,620 nautical miles at an average speed of ten knots. She was manned by a crew of 695, which, depending on operational requirements, would sometimes grow to as many as 775. She was 527 feet long with a beam of eighty-two feet and had an eight-inch to eleven-inch armour belt and eleven-inch armour on her five turrets, which mounted two twelve-inch guns each. Additional armament included twenty-seven twelve-pounder guns and five eighteen-inch torpedo tubes. Fully loaded, *Dreadnought* displaced 21,850 tons, quite similar to that of the current Royal Navy aircraft carrier HMS *Illustrious*.

Like many other prototypes, *Dreadnought* was not without faults, including a main belt armour that was too low, and inadequate anti-torpedo boat guns. But such flaws were not to be repeated in subsequent British dreadnoughts.

Britain was not alone in having concluded that the priorities for the next generation of battleships would be high speed and a unified primary armament of heavy guns with great size, range and accuracy. The planners and naval architects of the United States, Japan, and Italy were all busily developing their own versions of the new vessel while *Dreadnought* was being constructed. The U.S. was actually well ahead of Britain in such development, with their *South Carolina* class battleship at the time of *Dreadnought*'s keel laying. But *Dreadnought* was the first such ship afloat and with her arrival all other existing battleships became second rate.

An excellent image of HMS *Dreadnought* in her drydock.

In addition to *Dreadnought*, Fisher intended the development of a new armoured cruiser, the battlecruiser. He had wanted to use 9.2-inch guns in this class of warship, but in the end was persuaded that it should be armed with twelve-inch guns. The design was highly controversial in that, to achieve the required speed of twenty-five knots, a hull larger than that of *Dreadnought* was needed, and this, combined with the great weight of the big guns, made it necessary to save weight elsewhere by using the ordinary light armour of conventional armoured cruisers. HMS *Invincible* was the first ship of the new 'battlecruiser' class. She was followed in construction by sister-ships *Inflexible* and *Indomitable*. The keels for all three vessels were laid down in 1906 and all of them were completed in 1908. Like *Dreadnought*, the *Invincible* class battlecruisers were turbine-powered and were indeed capable of the twenty-five-knot requirement. They carried four turrets, each mounting two twelve-inch guns, but had only four to six-inch main belt armour, and seven-inch armour on the barbettes, giving them only minimal protection. *Invincible* was 567 feet long and displaced 17,370 tons. She had a top speed of 25.5 knots, a crew of 780 men and secondary armament of sixteen four-inch guns and five eighteen-inch torpedo tubes.

Just as Admiral Fisher's efforts were producing results, fears began to surface in Britain about Germany's rapidly expanding warship inventory. To this point the British had been quietly confident about their ability to outbuild and outgun the other significant fleets of the world, and in doing so, retain supremacy of the seas. Then in 1908, the Liberal British government decided to cut substantially the annual budget allocation for battleships. This immediately

HMS *Dreadnought* under way at sea.

sparked heated debate between the political parties about Britain's defence requirements and the associated costs. Economic reform was in the air and two British battleships under construction were cancelled. Concern at the Admiralty heightened when it was learned that the Germans were in fact accelerating their battleship construction effort, while the British were cutting back theirs. It appeared that the German battleship inventory could reach near parity with the British within three years. The argument continued in Parliament until the summer of 1909. The opposing factions in the Commons finally agreed on authorization for the building of four new dreadnoughts that year and four more in 1910, providing that German battleship construction continued at the current pace. Additionally, both Australia and New Zealand expressed concerns at the looming threat to British Commonwealth and naval supremacy and offered to pay for the construction of two new warships—battlecruisers—to be named *Australia* and *New Zealand*. The arms race between Britain and Germany in the run-up to the First World War resulted in construction by Britain of thirty-two battleships and ten battlecruisers. In that period, Germany built nineteen battleships and six battlecruisers. Many other nations caught battleship fever, spending vast sums to purchase their share of the perceived power and prestige associated with a fleet of these impressive new vessels. The naval inventories of France, Russia, the United States, Italy, Japan, Austria-Hungary, Brazil, Argentina and Chile all began to swell with the new warships. It was the battleship boom of all time.

With all her promise, the record of *Dreadnought* in World War One was not particularly impressive. In her entire combat career, she was credited with the destruction of just one enemy vessel, a German submarine, which she rammed and sank. Britain's dreadnought fleet proved to be a rather high-maintenance affair which, after only two months of wartime operation, required significant refitting in its various home ports, denying the Royal Navy the service of two or three of the vessels at any given time in the war. When hostilities ended, the British public was profoundly opposed to everything related to that conflict, not least the costly weaponry, and a massive programme of warship scrapping began. *Dreadnought* herself went to the breaker's yard in 1923.

Dreadnought's significance lay not in her war record, but in her profound influence on the navies of the world, which led to a sea change in their capital ship philosophies and planning.

Roll on, thou deep and dark blue ocean—roll! Ten thousand fleets sweep over thee in vain;
Man marks the earth with ruin—his control / Stops with the shore.
—from *Childe Harold's Pilgrimage* by Lord Byron

Nowhere else than upon the sea do the days, weeks, and months fall away quicker into the past. They seem to be left astern as easily as the light air bubbles in the swirls of the ship's wake.
—Joseph Conrad

Battle, n. A method of untying with the teeth a political knot that would not yield to the tongue.
—from *The Devil's Dictionary* by Ambrose Bierce

Jutland

"And, about this Jutland fight," I hinted, not for the first time. "Oh, that was just a fight. There was more of it than any other fight, I suppose, but I expect all modern naval actions must be pretty much the same." "But what does one do—how does one feel?" I insisted, though I knew it was hopeless. "One does one's job. Things are happening all the time. A man may be right under your nose one minute—serving a gun or something—and the next minute he isn't there." "And one notices that at the time?" "Yes, but there's no time to keep on noticing it. You've got to carry on somehow or other, or your show stops. I tell you what one does notice, though. If one goes below for anything, or has to pass through a flat somewhere, and one sees the old wardroom clock ticking, or a photograph pinned up, or anything of that sort, one notices that. Oh, yes, and there was another thing—the way a ship seemed to blow up if you were far off her. You'd see a glare, then a blaze, and then the smoke—miles high, lifting quite slowly. Then you'd get the row and the jar of it—just like bumping over submarines. Then, a long while after, perhaps, you run through a regular rain of bits of burnt paper coming down on the decks—like showers of volcanic ash, you know."
—from *Sea Warfare* by Rudyard Kipling, on the Battle of Jutland

HMS *Malaya*, a *Queen Elizabeth* Class battleship of the British Royal Navy, was launched in March 1915 and took part in the Battle of Jutland, 31 May 1916.

Designed and painted by Fred Spear, *Enlist* is among the most famous of recruiting posters.

On 31 May 1916, Vizeadmiral Reinhard Scheer, the German High Seas Fleet commander, ordered the deployment of Admiral Franz von Hipper's battlecruiser group from their North Sea ports. Scheer planned to entrap the British Grand Fleet, or as much of it as he could lure out of harbour. He sent the ships towards Norway in a bid to draw the British battlecruisers into intercepting his force. He then set out after his five battlecruisers with a force of twenty-two battleships, eleven cruisers, six pre-dreadnoughts and sixty-one torpedo boats. His plan called for U-boats to mine the routes the British vessels would take out of their bases at Cromarty, Rosyth and Scapa Flow. The subs were then to be stationed near the British bases in an attempt to torpedo the enemy dreadnoughts as they emerged. The U-boat captains were further assigned to report back to Scheer on all British warship movements in the area. Additional reconnaissance was to be carried out by Zeppelin airships, to keep Scheer informed of the size and position of the enemy force he would be facing.

The British had begun intercepting and reading German naval messages in 1914 after the onset of the First World War. On 16 May 1916, suspicion was aroused at the Admiralty in London when it was learned that several U-boats had left their usual stations along the Atlantic trade routes. The Admiralty discovered on 29 May that the German High Seas Fleet had been ordered to readiness for activity at sea on 31 May and 1 June.

As though in concert with Scheer's plan, British battlecruisers commanded by Admiral Sir David Beatty, promptly departed Rosyth to scout the area near Skagerrak Strait. They were then to steam to within seventy miles of the Grand Fleet, which was heading south from Scapa Flow under the command of Admiral John Jellicoe. Jellicoe had been ordered to take the fleet to an area roughly 100 miles east of Aberdeen. In the coming engagement with the enemy he was to report every movement to the operations room of the Admiralty, which would essentially run the battle from London. In the late evening of 30 May he led the fleet, in his flagship *Iron Duke*, from Scapa and positioned it on station at 2 p.m. the following day.

From the moment Beatty's battlecruisers left Rosyth, Scheer's scheme began to unravel. His U-boats did not manage to attack the enemy vessels as they cruised by, and with deteriorating weather in the area, the German airships were unable to operate. They flew later in the day, but, with minimal visibility, were of little use to Scheer who, at that point, lacked any up-to-date information about his opponents. He was unaware that the entire British fleet was bearing down on him as his High Seas Fleet took up their position. In another curious turn of events, the Admiralty apparently misinterpreted an intercepted German message and signalled Jellicoe at midday that Admiral Scheer's flagship, *Friedrich der Grosse*, had not left its Jade River moorings near Wilhelmshaven. The commanders of both the British and German fleets were thus unaware that they were converging on one another.

As it happened, Admiral Jellicoe's Grand Fleet had been directed to operate in the precise area where Admiral Hipper's battlecruisers were headed. The long-anticipated clash of the two great fleets was now inevitable. Fate seems to have intervened once again when, in the early afternoon, cruisers of both sides departed from their formations to investigate a distant sighting which turned out to be a Danish steamer. The opposing cruisers spotted one another while about fourteen miles apart and immediately set out to close that distance. At this point, both the German and British commanders believed that they were successfully luring their opposite number into a trap. The British cruisers *Galatea* and *Phaeton* approached

SMS *Ostfriesland* fought in the Battle of Jutland in 1916. She was one of four Helgoland class warships permitted to remain in Germany after the German defeat in World War One and was later transferred to the U.S. Navy. She was sunk during aerial bombing trials off the Virginia Capes in July 1921; right: The *Ostfriesland* in better days; lower left: German Admiral Franz von Hipper; lower right: Admiral Reinhard von Scheer.

and fired upon the German cruiser *Elbing*, which returned fire. *Galatea* sighted Hipper's battlecruisers and immediately signalled their approach to Admiral Beatty who promptly changed course, heading southeast.

The quality of reconnaissance for both sides continued to deteriorate. A British seaplane launched from the *Engadine*, was scouting in the area, trying to locate the main force of the enemy fleet. The crew only managed to spot the German cruisers. But in the next hour smoke columns from the British fleet were sighted by sailors on the German battlecruisers at the same moment that Beatty was receiving word about sightings of the German vessels from his ships. Beatty was eager for the confrontation and led a force of six battlecruisers into action against an enemy group of five such ships. He did not realize, however, that the main body of Admiral Scheer's High Seas Fleet was now bearing down on his force, as he and Hipper concentrated on outmanoeuvring one another over the next half hour. Beatty had changed course in an attempt to place his ships between Hipper's vessels and the German bases, while Hipper now swung his forces southeast, hoping to draw Beatty towards the German main force less than fifty miles away. The action was imminent and still neither Scheer nor Hipper knew that Jellicoe's main force was rapidly closing on them.

In the afternoon haze at 3:46 p.m., the seas and the weather were calm as the battle began in earnest. If either side had an initial advantage, it was the Germans, who had the sun behind

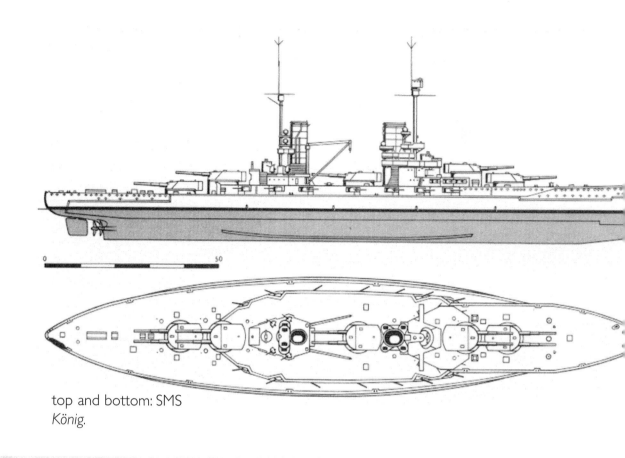

top and bottom: SMS
König.

below: SMS *Derfflinger* after he internment at Scapa Flow in 1919.

them, illuminating the enemy vessels and making their own ships more difficult to see. Almost as soon as the firing began, rolling black clouds of coal smoke combined with the haze to further obscure the combatants.

Hipper's flagship *Lutzow* was at the head of the German battlecruisers, leading *Derfflinger*, *Seydlitz*, *Moltke* and *Von der Tann*. Beatty's flagship *Lion*, was at the head of the British line of battlecruisers, and was followed by the *Princess Royal*, *Queen Mary*, *Tiger*, *New Zealand* and *Indefatigable*. *Lion* was hit immediately by shells from *Lutzow*, which hit a turret and killed the entire turret crew. *Lion's* magazines flooded and fires raged round the ship. By 4 p.m. the British battlecruisers had suffered several direct hits, while their German counterparts received just four. The most serious loss occurred when the *Von der Tann* hit HMS *Indefatigable* with three eleven-inch shells on her aft starboard quarter. Lurching out of line, the British vessel began to burn furiously as another shell from *Von der Tann* smashed into her forward twelve-inch gun turret, soon followed by yet another. Within seconds the stricken *Indefatigable* exploded in a massive orange fireball and sank rapidly by the stern, rolling over as she went, taking more than a thousand men down with her at 4.03 p.m. Only two of her crew survived.

By 4.25 p.m., the *Derfflinger* had the range of *Queen Mary* and scored hits on her, causing an immense explosion which forced HMS *Tiger*, the next ship in the line, to urgently change

above: HMS *Queen Mary* in port before Jutland; bottom: The last moments of the *Queen Mary* after her engagement with the German warships *Seydlitz* and *Derfflinger*.

course and dodge the wreck of *Queen Mary*. *Seydlitz* now joined the attack on *Queen Mary*, sending shells into her A and B magazines, which blew up with sufficient ferocity to tear the ship in two.

Petty Officer E. Francis, Ret., a survivor of HMS *Queen Mary*, described how he urged his shipmates to abandon ship: " 'Come on you chaps, who's coming for a swim?' Someone answered, 'She will float for a long time yet,' but something—I don't pretend to understand what it was—seemed to be urging me to get away, so I clambered up over the slimy bilge keel and fell off into the water, followed, I should think, by about five other men.

"I struck away from the ship as hard as I could, and must have covered nearly fifty yards, when there was a big smash, and stopping and looking round the air seemed to be full of fragments and flying pieces. A large piece seemed to be right above my head, and acting on impulse I dipped under to avoid being struck, and stayed under as long as I could, and then came to the top again, and coming behind me I heard a rush of water, which looked very much like a surf breaking on a beach, and I realised it was the suction or backwash from the ship, which had just gone down. I hardly had time to fill my lungs with air when it was on me; I felt it was no use struggling against it, so I let myself go for a moment or two, then struck out, but I felt it was a losing game, and remarked to myself, 'What's the use of you struggling, you're done,' and actually eased my efforts to reach the top, when a small voice seemed to say 'Dig out.'

"I started afresh, and something bumped against me. I grasped it and afterwards found it was a large hammock; it undoubtedly pulled me to the top, more dead than alive, and I rested on it, but I felt I was getting very weak and roused myself sufficiently to look around for something more subtantial to support me. Floating right in front of me was a piece of timber . . . I believe, the centre baulk of our Pattern 4 target. I managed to push myself on the hammock close to the timber and grasped a piece of rope hanging over the side. My next difficulty was to get on top, and with a small amount of exertion I kept on. I managed to reeve my arms through a stop, and then I must have become unconscious."

In only a few minutes *Queen Mary* went down with the loss of 1,285 men. There were nine survivors. Admiral Beatty now had just four battlecruisers remaining. The Germans still had five.

To the rescue now steamed four British *Queen Elizabeth* class battleships of the Fifth Battle Squadron, *Warspite*, *Barham*, *Valiant*, and *Malaya*, with fifteen-inch guns which were able to commence firing while still at a range of 19,000 yards. *Valiant* squared off against *Moltke* and *Barham* took on the *Von der Tann*. At such a great range the German ships could not respond and could only attempt to evade the British shells by changing course and zig-zagging. At this point Beatty needed time, pending the engagement of the entire Grand Fleet, and ordered a torpedo attack by his destroyers, causing Hipper to alter course. A twenty-one-inch British torpedo rent a great hole in the side of *Seydlitz*, which reduced her speed but did not force her to leave her position among the German battlecruisers. At last lookouts aboard one of Beatty's light cruisers spotted battleships of the High Seas Fleet twelve miles distant and signalled the admiral who brought his ships about in a feint as if to avoid engagement with the big German vessels. Actually, he was trying to coax them into proximity with the Grand Fleet. But sloppy communications left some of Beatty's ships in the dark about his intention and they soon found themselves within the range of the German fleet.

The four *Queen Elizabeth* class battleships slowly manoeuvred round to improve their positions relative to that of the enemy and, as they did, both *Barham* and *Malaya* were hit and incurred casualties. The four British vessels were firing too and soon were laying shells down on the *Markgraf*, *Grosser Kurfürst*, and the German battleships.

Describing his experiences in HMS *Malaya*, one of her sailors recalled: "I was Midshipman of the afternoon watch on May 31st, when a signal was received which seemed to excite the small crowd on 'Monkey's Island', the crew name for the upper bridge, from which the Captain or the Officer of the Watch controlled the ship, and being, like all snotties, very curious, I eventually mustered up enough courage to ask the Officer of the Watch what it was about, only to be snubbed for my pains. A few minutes later, however, the Captain sent me down to the Engineer Commander with a copy of a signal (which naturally, I suppose, I read). It was from the *Galatea*, reporting two enemy ships in sight. I duly returned to the bridge, after telling the Engineer Commander that the Captain wanted steam for full speed as soon as possible.

"I think we only realised that we were at last in for a proper action when we heard the battlecruisers firing ahead. We then began to get quite jubilant; so much so that when a German shell landed abreast us on the port side about 500 yards short, there was a positive cheer from the *Malaya*. Then we heard the other ships of our own squadron open fire, one after the other, ahead of us, each salvo helped on its way by a cheer. In our torpedo control tower we were so interested in what was going on, that when *Malaya* herself opened fire, the blast from 'X' turret's guns, which were only a few feet away from us, sat us down with a 'whump,' and the range taker came down from his seat with a crash.

"From this time onwards my thoughts were really more like a nightmare than thoughts of a wide-awake human being. I don't think I felt fright, simply because what was going on around me was so unfamiliar that my brain was incapable of grasping it. Even now I can only think of the beginning of the action as through a dim haze. I remember seeing the enemy line on the horizon with red specks coming out of them, which I tried to realise were the cause of projectiles landing around us, continually covering us with spray, but the fact refused to sink into my brain. We were all the time rather excited and our enthusiasm knew no bounds when we passed a sunken ship with survivors swimming around her. We never dreamt that it was one of our own battlecruisers; but it was the *Indefatigable*, and over a thousand dead men lay in her wreck. The same thing occurred when we passed the wreckage and survivors of the *Queen Mary*. Even when a man on some wreckage waved to us, we thought it must be a German wanting to be picked up. It is rather dreadful to think of now, especially as some men were not too keen on rescuing Germans after the *Lusitania* and similar atrocities, but I have often thought since how well it showed the confidence that we had in our own fleet that no one for a moment imagined that one of our own ships would be sunk so soon.

"All this time I was gradually getting my thoughts out of their 'dreamy' state, and was slowly beginning to realise that all these projectiles falling a few yards short and over were big ones, and that they were meant for us; and my thoughts, following their natural course, led me on to think of my life-saving waistcoat which, like a fool, I had left in my seachest down below. There was no chance of getting it now.

"All this time we were being thrown about by the blast of 'X' turret, and we spent quite

46

above left: Admiral David Beatty; above right: Admiral John Jellicoe; below: HMS *Iron Duke*, the flagship of Admiral Jellicoe at Jutland.

H.M.S. IRON DUKE, 1st Fleet Flagship

Commissioned in 1914, the U.S.Navy
battleship USS *New York* was typical of
American battleships of the World War
One era.

a portion of our time in ungraceful and rather painful positions on the deck, bumping against the range-finder, plotter and other things with sharp corners.

"Shortly after 7:30 p.m. we lost touch altogether with the enemy, and a lull in the action occurred. After having a look at the damage done to X turret, I went forward and was surprised to see a large shell hole in the upper deck near No 3 six-inch gun starboard. The lower boom stanchion was buckled out of all recognition and the bread store was a twisted heap of wreckage. I went down to the battery, where everything was dark chaos. Most of the wounded had been taken away but several of the killed were still there. The most ghastly part of the whole affair was the smell of burnt flesh, which remained in the ship for weeks, making everybody have a sickly nauseous feeling the whole time. When the battery was finally lighted by an emergency circuit, it was a scene which cannot easily be forgotten—everything burnt black and bare from the fire; the galley, canteen, and drying room bulkheads blown and twisted into the most grotesque shapes, and whole deck covered by about six inches of water and dreadful debris, and permeating everywhere the awful stench of cordite fumes and of war. It is hardly surprising that the nerves of many of us were shaken, especially as the men below decks and in other stations away from the actual damage had never dreamt that we had suffered such damage or casualties.

"By the time it was dark we were all at our stations again. Some of the torpedo control tower's crew were lying on the deck, whilst the remainder kept a lookout."

As the ships of the British Grand Fleet steamed south to join Beatty's battlecruiser force which was still heading north, Admiral Jellicoe ordered three of his *Invincible* class battlecruisers, under the command of Rear Admiral Sir Horace Hood, to go to the aid of Beatty. After the various course reversals of both sides, the situation was now that Hipper's force was leading the entire German High Seas Fleet, pursuing Beatty's battlecruisers northwards, and steaming into the arms of the Grand Fleet; all seemed set for the confrontation that the British had been seeking since the start of the war.

At 5:26 p.m. the light was changing as Beatty halted the northerly run of his ships to turn and re-engage Hipper. Now the advantage of illumination began to be with the British, who capitalized on it, badly damaging *Lutzow*. *Derfflinger* was starting to take on water due to severe bow damage and *Seydlitz* was afire. All the big guns of *Von der Tann* had been put out of action and Admiral Hipper was forced to bring his destroyers up in a desperate attack on the British line. It was then that Hood's three battlecruisers arrived to scatter the German destroyers.

Once again a situation arose in which optimal intelligence based on thorough, up-to-the-minute reconnaissance was required by both sides. Information of this quality, however, was simply not available. Admiral Jellicoe, probably the best naval tactician in the world at the time of Jutland, had just seven miles visibility from the bridge of *Iron Duke* and knew very little about the present position, speed and bearing of the enemy fleet. He did know that he had only a few moments to deploy the vessels of the Grand Fleet in such a way as to allow all their big guns to bear on the enemy as soon as they came within range. He quickly ordered the fleet to form a nine-mile-long single column. The move positioned his newest and most capable battleships to initiate the action, and was, according to most naval historians, probably the most effective deployment anyone could have achieved in the circumstances. As he completed the manoeuvre, Jellicoe's fleet was joined by the British battlecruisers.

In the relatively shallow water of the Jutland Bank off the coast of Denmark, sailors of the Grand Fleet witnessed a grotesque spectacle in the aftermath of an attack by *König* and *Derfflinger* on HMS *Invincible*. In the waning sunlight, *Invincible*, the flagship of Admiral Hood, was struck by a massive salvo that destroyed her mid-ships turrets, sending fire into the magazines below, setting off an enormous explosion that broke her hull in two. Both halves of the 570-foot-long battlecruiser then sank vertically, leaving the bow and stern standing out of the water like gravestones. Of her crew, 1,026 men died. Just six were saved.

The two great battle fleets now engaged in a series of gun actions. Jellicoe and the Grand Fleet crossed the 'T' of Scheer's High Seas Fleet and the German ships began to receive the full firepower of the British battleship line. It was Scheer who was trapped. His only option was a 180 degree "battle turnaway." All the German battleships accomplished the manoeuvre and, in the gathering mist of early evening, aided by a smokescreen laid by his destroyers, Scheer's force retreated.

At 6:56 p.m. Jellicoe had brought the Grand Fleet round to the south to cut off Scheer's escape route and, at 7:08, Scheer's T was crossed again, exposing his ships to an even more devastating assault from the British battleships. What followed has been referred to as "the death ride" of the German battlecruisers. Scheer ordered them to "Charge the enemy. Ram. Ships denoted are to attack without regard to consequences." Leading the ride was *Derfflinger*,

THE SEMAPHORE ALPHABET.

CHAR-ACTERS	HAND FLAGS	CHAR-ACTERS	HAND FLAGS	CHAR-ACTERS	HAND FLAGS	CHAR-ACTERS	HAND FLAGS
A		I		Q		Y	
B		J		R		Z	
C OR ANSWER-ING SIGN		K		S		ATTEN-TION	
D		L		T		FRONT	
E OR ERASE SIGN		M		U			
F		N		V			
G		O		W			
H		P		X			

The German High Seas Fleet
in May 1916.

which quickly lost her fire control and two turrets in the ensuing action. *Lutzow* was hit and burned furiously. *Seydlitz* took five hits. In this phase of the battle, only two Grand Fleet ships suffered significant damage. *Colossus* was struck by two shells and *Marlborough* received a torpedo, but both ships were able to carry on. Firing continued until 8:35, but by then the main fleet action of Jutland was finished. Through the night, German battleships continued to fire on British cruisers and destroyers near the rear of the Grand Fleet. Jellicoe, however, was loath to risk substantial night action, fearing the liklihood of mistakes in ship identification as well as collision. Scheer, for his part, could not afford such reservations and took the risk in order to shepherd his fleet back to the safety of Wilhelmshaven. Only his pre-dreadnought *Pommern*, which blew up when struck by a British torpedo, and *Lutzow*, which had to be sunk by German destroyers when she could no longer maintain steam, were lost in the effort. On their return to Wilhelmshaven, *Seydlitz* and *Derfflinger* had both lost half their armament. Hipper led them back in *Moltke*.

The eminent British historian Sir John Keegan has written of the Battle: "By comparison with the losses suffered in contemporary battles on land—Verdun and the Somme, both fought in 1916—Jutland was not costly. The total number of sailors killed was 8,500, about 6,000 British, 2,500 German. It is the manner of dying that apalls. Burns, rarely suffered in trench warfare, were a major cause of death, usually the result of boilers bursting or cordite catching fire. The doctors were bewildered by the symptoms. Often the victims seemed scarcely hurt at first but then displayed strange signs of deterioration and died within the day. Shell splinter wounds varied in nature, from multiple pepperpotting to decapitation. What sailors feared most was drowning inside the ship. Shut in small compartments behind watertight

doors, they could be overcome by a high-pressure gush through a shell hole. The quickest end was by the detonation of a main magazine, which destroyed the ship, the cause of the loss of *Indefatigable*, *Invincible*, and *Queen Mary*."

Jutland was basically a draw. The German forces had sunk three British capital ships and three armoured cruisers. The British had sunk one capital ship and one elderly battleship. On the day after the battle, the British had possession of the 'battlefield' and their Grand Fleet returned to its ports largely intact. It was refuelled, rearmed and essentially ready to put to sea again a day later.

In terms of the total numbers of men and ships lost, the German claim to victory was justified. The British lost fourteen ships, the Germans eleven. Personnel losses amounted to 6,097 British and 2,551 German. Strategically, Britain's Grand Fleet still ruled the North Sea and the British still maintained their blockade of Germany. Technologically, the Germans had the edge with their big gun shells, which were filled with desensitized TNT (trinitrotoluene), a considerable improvement over the Lyddite-filled shells of the British. Certainly, both sides suffered from grossly inadequate communications.

The vast investment in ships and men which both sides had made during the pre-war naval race had not brought to either the dividends which it had hoped for. The Royal Navy had failed to achieve the decisive victory which it sought, and would never get another chance to defeat the Germans in a fleet action. The grandly named High Seas Fleet, on the other hand, was now reduced to the role of a coastal defence force and acting as an adjunct to the less visually impressive but far more effective U-boat fleet.

With the Armistice of 1918, Germany lost her status as a great naval power. Under the

terms of the peace Treaty of Versailles, her fleet was interned. In November 1918, the High Seas Fleet sailed from Wilhelmshaven to the Firth of Forth in Scotland, and later to its final destination, Scapa Flow. For months the Allies continued to discuss the ultimate fate of the German ships which lay at anchor in Scapa. The ships were in the care of German skeleton crews, overseen by British armed guards. With the Armistice due to expire on 21 June 1919, when the Treaty of Versailles came into effect, the German commander of the interned fleet, Vizeadmiral Ludwig von Reuter, took matters into his own hands. At mid-morning on the 21st Reuter ordered his crews to scuttle the ships.

In the next two decades most of the former German warships were raised from the waters of Scapa Flow and towed to Rosyth and elsewhere in Britain where they were eventually broken up for scrap. The battleships *Kronprinz*, *Markgraf*, and *König* remain at the bottom of Scapa to this day.

Hit your enemy in the belly, and kick him when he is down, and boil his prisoners in oil—if you take any—and torture his women and children. Then people will keep clear of you.
—Admiral of the Fleet Lord Fisher, addressing the Hague Peace Conference of 1899.

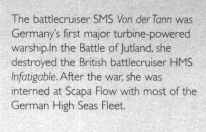

"I was surprised to find that in addition to being able to follow the flight of one's own projectiles with spotting glasses, the enemy's projectiles also appeared as dots getting larger and larger, till they burst short or droned past and fell beyond us. They always seemed to be coming straight for one's eyes. Ricochets were also clearly visible, turning end over end, and making a noise like the rumbling of a distant train."
—an officer of HMS *New Zealand*

"The *Queen Mary* was next ahead of us, and I remember watching her for a little, and saw one salvo straddle her. Three shells out of four hit, and the impression one got of seeing the splinters fly and the dull red burst was as if no damage had been done, but that the armour was keeping the shell out. The next salvo that I saw straddled her, and two more shells hit her. As they hit, I saw a dull red glow amidships, and then the ship seemed to open out like a puff ball, or one of those toadstool things when one squeezes it. Then there was another dull red glow somewhere forward, and the whole ship seemed to collapse inwards. The funnels and masts fell into the middle and the hull was blown outwards. The roofs of the turrets were blown 100 feet high, then everything was smoke, and a bit of the stern was the

only part of the ship left above water. The *Tiger* put her helm hard-a-starboard, and we just cleared the remains of the *Queen Mary*'s stern by a few feet."
—an officer in HMS *Tiger*

"There seems to be something wrong with our bloody ships today."
—Admiral Sir David Beatty at the Battle of Jutland

"For all that has been said of the love that certain natures (on shore) have professed to feel for it, for all the celebrations it has been the object of in prose and song, the sea has never been friendly to man. At most it has been the accomplice of human restlessness." —Joseph Conrad

At Jutland, HMS *Barham* served with Admiral Beatty's battlecruiser fleet. In the late afternoon of 25 November 1941, *Barham* was helping the battleships *Queen Elizabeth* and *Valiant* cover an attack on Italian convoys when she was sunk by three torpedoes from the U-boat *U-331*.

Between the Wars

Anxious to take advantage of a peace dividend at the end of the First World War, Britain quickly scrapped nearly 400 of her warships, among them forty capital ships. An expansionist Japan, meanwhile, was growing her warship fleet at a rapid pace, with considerable British support. In response to the Japanese naval construction programme, the Americans began building four *Maryland* class battleships; 32,500-ton vessels armed with eight sixteen-inch guns, to counter the new, similarly-armed *Nagato* class battleships of Japan. By 1921 the United States had a total of twelve battleships under construction. The British fell behind the battleship curve and did not join this arms race until 1925 when they authorized construction of four new 46,000-ton battlecruisers. They were unable to finance a further four capital ships—48,500-ton battleships to be armed with eighteen-inch guns.

In 1921 the administration of the new U.S. president Warren G. Harding, sponsored a major conference on arms limitation held at Washington. The conference led to a treaty in 1922 by which the five main naval powers, the United States, Britain, France, Italy, and Japan, agreed to limit capital ship tonnages as follows: Britain and the United States were each confined to a total of 525,000 tons, Japan was entitled to 315,000 tons, while France and Italy could each have 175,000 tons. Individual capital ships would be limited to a maximum of 35,000 tons with armament no larger than sixteen-inch guns. Britain and the United States would be limited to a total aircraft carrier tonnage of 135,000, with new carriers limited to an individual tonnage of 27,000. All lesser warships would be limited to 10,000 tons each with guns no larger than eight-inch calibre.

The Treaty of Versailles, signed on 28 June 1919, had decreed that Germany's future armoured warships could not exceed a displacement of 10,000 tons, with cruisers limited to 6,000 tons, and destroyers to 800 tons. Submarines and military aircraft were entirely prohibited.

Germany sought ways around the Versailles terms which it saw as excessively restrictive. It initiated clandestine projects such as a design bureau in the Netherlands that employed former wartime U-boat designers. The bureau was actually working for the German Admiralty, designing and supervising the construction of submarines for Turkey, Spain, and Finland. These designs would later be utilized in the production of German U-boats for use in World War Two. In another move to circumvent the Versailles rules, the Germans developed the design for an 'armoured ship', the Panzerschiff, or pocket battleship. It would, in fact, exceed the 10,000-ton limitation by twenty-three per cent and be armed with six eleven-inch guns and eight 5.9-inch guns. Its diesel engines gave it a speed of twenty-six knots, faster than most battleships of the time. By 1934, the Germans had completed three of the pocket battleships.

In a climate of austerity in the United States, the administration of President Herbert Hoover cut the pace of warship construction, planning, and funding. By 1930, the U.S. was at the rear of the inventory and building race with only eleven such vessels completed or under construction. Leading the category was Japan with 125. Then came France with 119, followed by Italy with eighty-two and Britain with seventy-four. In the background, Germany continued to rearm in secret.

Franklin D. Roosevelt was elected president of the United States in 1932 and, in the midst

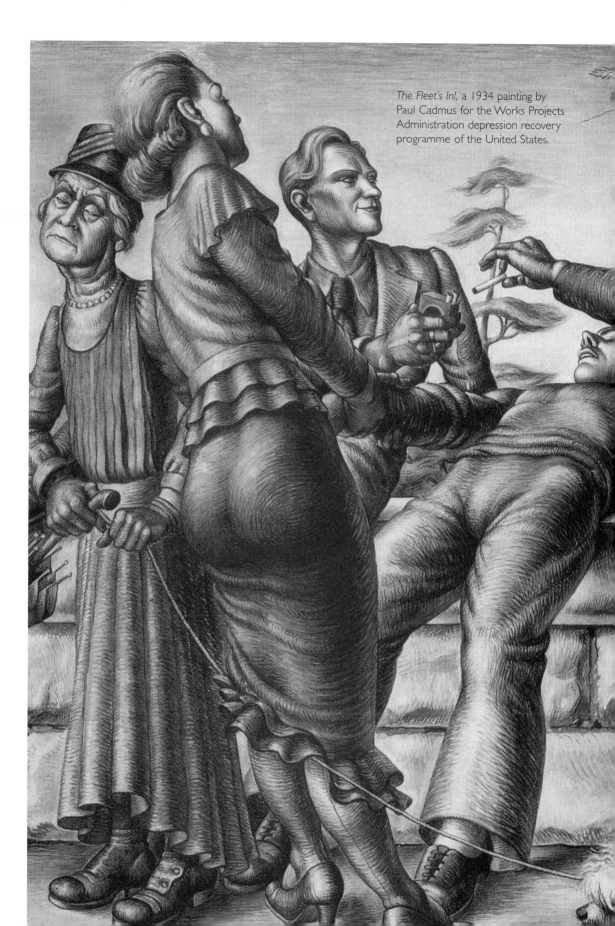

The Fleet's In!, a 1934 painting by Paul Cadmus for the Works Projects Administration depression recovery programme of the United States.

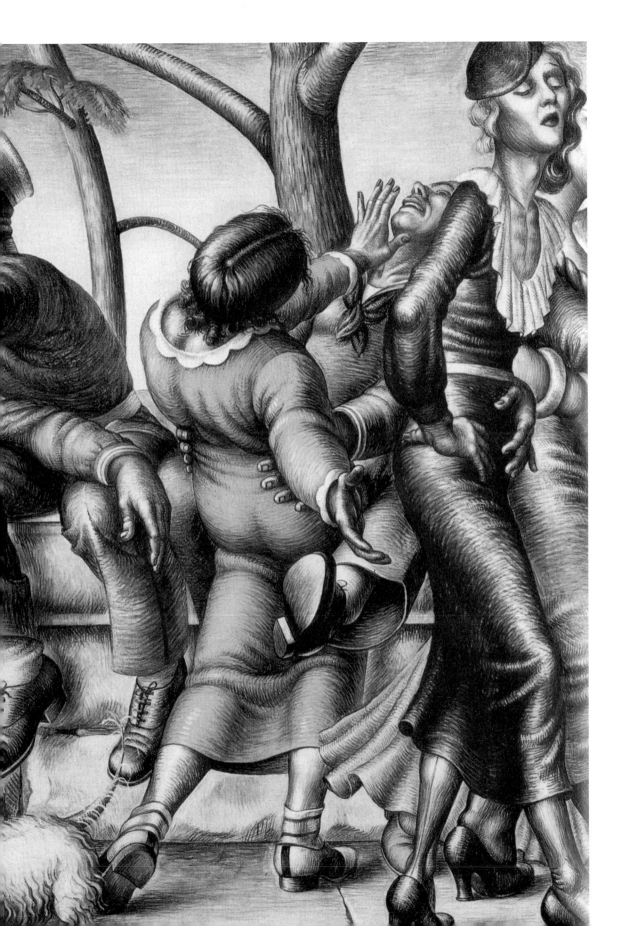

of the Great Depression era, presided over new funding for warship construction as part of the National Industrial Recovery Act approved by the Congress.

In January 1933, Adolf Hitler became Chancellor of Germany and, by 1934, had joined Japan in withdrawing from the League of Nations. Japan and Germany were flouting the dictates of Versailles and later the Washington and London naval conferences. Hitler took the further illegal step of reintroducing conscription in Germany. France and Italy, both concerned about German pocket battleship development, began construction in the early 1930s of the *Dunkerque* and *Vittorio Veneto* class battleships, respectively—and the Germans started work on *Scharnhorst* and *Gneisenau* in 1935. In an effort to catch up with the other nations and counter the Japanese warship building programme, Roosevelt spearheaded the 1934 Vinson-Trammell Act which authorized work on approximately 100 new warships.

By the mid-thirties, Britain's warship fleet was largely in poor shape, run-down and mostly obsolete. Forming the core of the fleet were the remaining *Queen Elizabeth* and *Revenge* or R class battleships, and the *Hood*. Planned in response to the four German *Mackensen* class battlecruisers of 1914, the 46,000-ton *Hood* was completed in 1920, the only one of her class of four battlecruisers to reach completion. The 34,000-ton *Nelson* and *Rodney* joined the fleet in 1927 as the first battleships to be designed to the newly-imposed 35,000-ton limit. Meanwhile, flagrantly disregarding the treaty terms that bound her, Germany was building U-boats and rapidly rearming. In addition to submarines, her shipyards were hard at work on the design and construction of six new capital ships, at least one carrier, eighteen cruisers and dozens of destroyers.

At another conference of the big five naval powers, held in London in 1935, Japan insisted that she would not be bound by the Washington Treaty limitations. The head of the Imperial Japanese Navy, Admiral Isoroku Yamamoto, proposed the total abolition of the battleship. "These ships are like elaborate religious scrolls which old people hang up in their homes. They are purely a matter of faith, not reality. The battleship is as useful in modern warfare as a samurai sword." The other conferees rejected his proposal and the Japanese withdrew from the talks. The naval treaties that had helped keep the peace were unravelling.

A so-called London Protocol of the time found Britain and Germany agreeing that submarines were bound by international law not to attack merchant ships without warning. Britain's 1930s policy of non-alienation served to embolden Hitler, and Italy's Benito Mussolini, in their territorial adventurism. The United States felt embittered that the European nations appeared to be throwing away the hard-won peace after World War One, and the American people turned more and more isolationist as the decade wore on. In 1936, Germany began work on the battleships *Bismarck* and *Tirpitz*, both of which would greatly exceed their officially allowed displacement and, in this uneasy world climate, Japan was busy planning construction of the 67,000-ton *Yamato* class battleship which would out-range and out-gun any warship afloat. With eighteen-inch guns, they would be the largest, most powerful and deadly battleships ever built.

When Ohio inventors and bicycle repairmen Orville and Wilbur Wright managed to fly their odd-looking machine at Kill Devil Hill near Kitty Hawk, North Carolina in December 1903, the event attracted relatively little interest. Mankind's first successful attempt at powered flight did not impress the American government of the time. Still, the Wrights went on with their aerial experimentation, attracting far less attention than they deserved. After rejection by their own government, they offered their invention to Britain, where the War Office and Admiralty turned them down three times. In France during 1908, however, they met a very different reaction when they put their flying machine through an exciting one-and-a-half-hour display. By then, Britain, Russia, and much of Europe had awakened to the military potential of aircraft.

On 14 November 1910, an American aviator named Eugene Ely coaxed his fifty-horse-power Glenn Curtiss biplane from a short platform built on the cruiser *Birmingham*, in history's first "carrier launch" of an aircraft. Two months later, Ely executed the first carrier landing on the 120-foot deck platform of the cruiser *Pennsylvania*. Less than a year later, he died in a crash during one of his demonstration flights. Of his achievements, the British magazine *Aeroplane*, 25 January 1911, commented: ". . . this partakes too much of the nature of trick flying to be of much practical value. A naval aeroplane would be of more use if it 'landed' on the water and could then be hauled on board. A slight error in steering when trying to alight on deck would wreck the whole machine." By 1911, following many trials, aircraft were being successfully launched from flimsy tracks erected on the forward turret of British battleships.

By 1912 the Royal Flying Corps was established in Britain, with the intention of providing both military and naval aviators and aircraft to support their respective services in a war. Experimentation into the possible offensive use of naval aircraft for the delivery of bombs and torpedoes soon began. In 1913, British trials involving a Short seaplane dropping a torpedo were successfully carried out, and in America, Glenn Curtiss was achieving considerable accuracy in dropping bombs on "warship" targets from his planes.

Britain's naval air capability steadily increased from 1914 onwards. When the First World War started, the Royal Navy was operating one seaplane carrier, thirty-nine aeroplanes and fifty-two seaplanes; by the end of the war in 1918, her naval and land air forces mustered eleven carriers, 3,000 land and seaplanes and more than fifty non-rigid airships, with 55,000 personnel.

German air strength by the end of the war included nearly 700 seaplanes, 190 land planes, and seven airships. Entering the war with only a handful of aircraft and personnel, the United States Navy emerged from it with nearly 1,900 flying boats and seaplanes, and more than 50,000 men. The first aerial attack on warships occurred on Christmas Day 1914, when German seaplanes and Zeppelins dropped bombs on British ships which had attempted an attack on the Zeppelin sheds at Cuxhaven in northern Germany. Neither the planes nor the Zeppelins succeeded in hitting a ship.

In all of the First World War, no warships were seriously damaged or sunk by aircraft and only a few merchant ships were destroyed or seriously damaged in such attacks.

Proponents and opponents of naval aviation after World War One engaged in a debate that had begun after the Battle of Jutland and would continue throughout the 1920s and 1930s. The British Admiralty was not at all enthusiastic about developing a naval air arm. It viewed the aircraft carrier with suspicion, just as it had regarded the submarine a decade earlier. The first aircraft carriers, existing vessels converted to launch and recover aircraft, were perceived as too slow to keep up with the capital ships of the Fleet. It was not until 1923 that HMS *Hermes*, the world's first purpose-built aircraft carrier, was completed. Even then, few in the Royal Navy were keen about expanding the role of aviation for their service. This

A scene from the movie *The Court-Martial of Billy Mitchell* in which the American officer is tried for publicly complaining about the High Command's neglect of the aerial fighting forces.

lack of enthusiasm in naval circles had contributed to the government decision to form an independent Royal Air Force in 1918. Relatively few naval people accepted that aviation served any useful naval function beyond reconnaissance duties.

The Navy and War Departments of the U.S. government were separately administered and were heatedly involved in the debate. The prime advocate of strategic bombing by fixed-wing aircraft as an ultimate war-winning policy was Brigadier General William 'Billy' Mitchell. In his opinion, if aircraft were "allowed to develop essential air weapons, [they could] carry war to such an extent . . . as almost to make navies useless on the surface of the water." Mitchell wanted to prove to the Navy, the nation and the world that accurate aerial bombing of an enemy nation's capital ships was feasible and that aircraft would play a decisive role in future naval warfare. A series of trials was agreed with the Navy and scheduled to begin

THE SHIPS ARE COMING

UNITED STATES SHIPPING BOARD ▪ EMERGENCY FLEET CORPORATION

THE TIDAL WAVE

JULY 4, 1918

95 Ships Launched

UNITED STATES SHIPPING BOARD EMERGENCY FLEET CORPORATION

THE NAVY NEEDS YOU! DON'T **READ** AMERICAN HISTORY— **MAKE IT !**

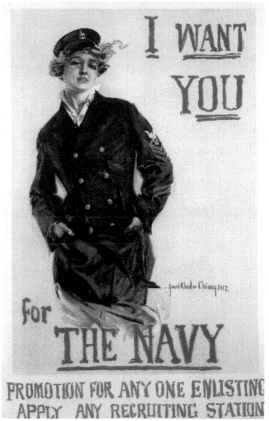

I WANT YOU

for THE NAVY

PROMOTION FOR ANY ONE ENLISTING
APPLY ANY RECRUITING STATION

BRITISHERS

THE HEGEMAN PRINT N.Y.

ENLIST TO·DAY

in 1921. Former enemy warships were to be the targets of Mitchell's bomber and the ships were to be boarded between bombing tests so that the damage caused by the bombing could be assessed. Mitchell wanted to make the trials as high-profile as possible, for maximum publicity value, and was less concerned with a scrupulous adherence to the rules of the tests than with his planes sinking battleships. Though he established an early precedent when his 2,000-pound bombs quickly sank the *Ostfriesland*, this only proved that an old German battleship at anchor, with no active anti-aircraft guns and no damage control, could be sunk by bombers.

The argument continued. The conventional conservative wisdom in the British and American navies held that, whether or not Mitchell was correct, a navy's first responsibility was to be prepared to fight wars in the present and not to concentrate all its resources on preparing for the future. Mitchell and his supporters, on the other hand, argued that, it having been shown (at least to the satisfaction of some) that bombers could sink battleships, it followed that in the next war, all the battleships involved would be sunk by bombers, as would all the aircraft carriers. Both sides were, of course, wrong. Battleships would prove to be dangerously vulnerable to bombers, but the bombers that did most of the damage came not from land bases but from carriers. In fact, during World War Two, very few battleships succombed to attack by shore-based bombers. In excess of 200 aircraft carriers participated in that war and only one was actually sunk by shore-based bombers.

In the experimental bombing runs by aircraft under the command of General Billy Mitchell, who used these tests to support his ideas that the battleships were obsolete in the face of air power, the first USS *New Jersey*, BB16, was sunk off Cape Hatteras, North Carolina on 5 September 1922.

"The long day finished with us slinging our hammocks, holding the 'nettles' [strings] open at our headends with a short stick, unfolding our heavy woolen blankets lengthways across our hammock before swinging our bodies in; a comfortable bed with our boots and clothing made into a pillow. We soon got used to it, as we did to the ever-present hum of fan motors pushing stale air from one compartment to the next, and the subdued roar of machinery. The lights were not dimmed until 'lights out' at 10 o'clock. The first night, fitful sleep came to most after a lot of wriggling about, trying to keep our blankets wrapped around us at the same time, and attempting to ignore the bright overhead light. Our long troubled night, broken by odd bumps underneath as passers-by 'headed' our hammocks, as they went about their duties, was ended by the switching on of all lights and raucous shouting of the duty Petty Officer. The time being 5:30 gave us little time to lash up and stow our hammocks, get dressed and find our promised cup of Kye [cocoa] and ship's bisquit. The established mess mates had turned out early to draw the rations in comfort. We were only caught the once, as like all things learned the hard way, only fools get caught twice. The next day we mustered at 6 o'clock, still trying to crunch the hard ship's biscuit before someone robbed us of it. On mustering, the Duty Officer gave the usual orders to scrub the decks. That morning in the unusually cold weather for Portsmouth, the sea water turned to icy slush as it was hosed on to the deck.
—a sailor in HMS *Hood*, from *The Royal Navy in The Second World War* by Julian Thompson

A still from the Rank Organisation film *Pursuit of the Graf Spee*, with Anthony Quale, Peter Finch, and John Gregson.

In 1912, at the age of eighteen, Hans Wilhelm Langsdorff enlisted in the Imperial German Navy. He saw front-line action four years later in the Battle of Jutland and soon afterward was placed in command of a minesweeper. In the 1920s, he commanded a flotilla of torpedo boats and then, in the early '30s, served for four years in Berlin at the Ministry of Defence. By 1938 he held the rank of Kapitän zur See and was given command of the pocket battleship *Admiral Graf Spee*.

Admiral Graf Spee and her sister ships *Admiral Scheer* and *Deutschland*, were the pride of the new German Navy in the 1930s. With their high-speed diesel-powered performance, and their eleven-inch guns, they commanded considerable respect from the world's other naval powers. Their relatively light belt and deck armour, however, made them more vulnerable than they seemed. In their design they appeared to conform to the restrictions of the Versailles Treaty, but they clearly exceeded the treaty-imposed weight restrictions.

Graf Spee sailed from her berth in Wilhelmshaven on 21 August 1939, a few days before the outbreak of war with Britain, for the South Atlantic. The voyage would be known as her 'raider cruise'. Her assignment was to hunt, attack and sink merchant vessels plying the vital shipping lanes to Britain. From 30 September to early December, she sank nine British freighters—a total of 50,000 tons.

Unlike many commanders who followed him, Captain Langsdorff was a strict adherent to the dictates of the Hague Conventions. He ensured that *Graf Spee* displayed her battle ensign when she encountered a ship to be attacked, and signalled a clear warning to the merchant crew: STOP. DO NOT USE WIRELESS OR WE WILL FIRE. He saw that the merchant crew were taken off their vessels before his crew sank them. Not one of the sixty-two prisoners he took from the merchant ships sunk by *Graf Spee* was harmed.

On the morning of 13 December 1939, a lookout in *Graf Spee* sighted a ship in the distance and Captain Langsdorff ordered his helmsman to pursue the vessel to identify it. They were about 200 miles off the estuary of the River Plate, which separates Uruguay from Argentina, on the east coast of South America. As the pocket battleship closed in on the potential prey, it was identified as the French liner *Formose*. Just then another ship was sighted from *Graf Spee*. It was the Royal Navy cruiser HMS *Exeter*, which had heard radio distress calls from *Formose* and was steaming to her assistance. The *Exeter* signalled two light cruisers which were then hunting for *Graf Spee*, HMS *Ajax* and HMNZS *Achilles*, which hurried to join her. As the cruisers approached the area, *Graf Spee* turned on a southerly course. *Formose* had changed course and departed.

Captain Langsdorff, his ship low on fuel, preferred to avoid combat with the British warships and altered course to evade them, but he soon noted that the *Ajax* and *Achilles* were approaching and cutting off his escape route from *Exeter*. His only option was to stand and fight. He hoped to destroy *Exeter* before the other cruisers arrived, and began firing his eleven-inch guns before the British ship with her eight inch guns was in range to return fire. One shell struck *Exeter*'s bridge with devastating effect, killing all present but the captain, another officer and one midshipman. Seriously damaged, with fires below decks, three feet down by the bows and shipping water forward, *Exeter* was a ruin, but she was soon within range and began firing salvos at the German warship. Another shell from *Graf Spee* caused her to slow dramatically, but she maintained position to block any attempt by the German ship to escape to the north. By mid-day, however, the badly damaged British cruiser had to retire from the action, leaving it to *Ajax and Achilles*.

In his book, Langsdorff of the *Graf Spee, Prince of Honour*, Joseph Gilbey writes: "There is little to compare to the hellish brutality of a sea battle. Men are entrapped in a tight steel box, a warship. They are beyond sight of land, floating in untold fathoms of sea-water. Separated by miles of rolling ocean, combatting warships throwing tons of high explosives at each other. It seems an unreal fantasy. Eventually, like a thunderbolt, a shell pierces the ship. A deafening explosion sends lethal particles of shrapnel and flying debris ricocheting off the ship's interior panels. Unfortunate men are cut down instantly in death or mutilation. Fire, fumes, and flooding in darkened confined spaces summon terror to the survivors. Exercises can never equal the real thing."

Ajax and Achilles, both armed with six-inch guns, had sandwiched *Graf Spee* and, under cover of smoke screens, were firing at the German warship from both sides, causing considerable damage. Captain Langsdorff decided to break off the action and headed out to sea, but the British cruisers gave chase and, leaving the smoke screens behind, closed to within a mile of the German vessel. *Graf Spee* was being savaged by the close-range attack and turned westward, laying a smoke screen as she manoeuvred. Langsdorff signalled the German Admiralty: "I HAVE TAKEN FIFTEEN HITS. FOOD STORES AND GALLEYS DESTROYED. I AM HEADING FOR MONTEVIDEO". The *Graf Spee* was followed closely by *Achilles*. Both British cruisers had suffered in the action and few of their bigger guns were still functioning. *Ajax* and *Achilles* took positions off the estuary that evening as *Graf Spee* entered the harbour.

The German pocket battleship *Graf Spee* was launched in 1936.

Captain Langsdorff requested that the authorities in Montevideo grant him fifteen days to repair his ship and make her seaworthy again. They gave him seventy-two hours, during which his sixty wounded were treated and the thirty-six dead were taken off the ship for burial. The British Admiralty, meanwhile, had dispatched a fourth cruiser, HMS *Cumberland*, to join the other three and to await the German's next move.

Langsdorff believed, incorrectly, that the Royal Navy aircraft carrier *Ark Royal* and the battlecruiser *Renown* had come to the aid of *Ajax* and *Achilles*. He sent the following signal to Admiral Raeder in Berlin on 16 December: "APART FROM THE BRITISH CRUISERS AND DESTROYERS, THE AIRCRAFT CARRIER ARK ROYAL AND THE BATTLECRUISER RENOWN HAVE JOINED THE NAVAL FORCES TO TIGHTLY BLOCK OUR ESCAPE ROUTE. NO PROSPECT OF BREAKING OUT INTO THE OPEN SEA OR REACHING HOME. PROPOSE EMERGING AS FAR AS NEUTRAL WATERS LIMIT AND ATTEMPT TO FIGHT THROUGH TO BUENOS AIRES USING REMAINING AMMUNITION. BREAKOUT WOULD RESULT IN CERTAIN DESTRUCTION OF GRAF SPEE WITH NO CHANCE OF DAMAGING ENEMY SHIPS. REQUEST DECISION WHETHER TO SCUTTLE DESPITE INADEQUATE DEPTH OF WATER OR ACCEPT INTERNMENT." After conferring on the matter with Hitler, Raeder signalled Langsdorff that the *Graf Spee* was to remain at Montevideo for as long as authorities there would allow; a breakout to Buenos Aires was approved, but internment in Uruguay was not. If scuttling was necessary, everything in the ship was to be thoroughly destroyed. From Langsdorff of the *Graf Spee*, *Prince of Honour*. "As the hours ticked away, the world waited. A blood-bath seemed certain. Tension mounted

far left: The *Graf Spee* was under the command of Captain Hans Langsdorff; below: SMS *Graf Spee*.

at 6:45 p.m. when a black cloud of smoke puffed out of *Graf Spee's* funnel. Slowly, amid the rattle of heavy chains, the forward anchor rose out of black, sucking mud. Idling diesels revved into powerful life. *Graf Spee* swung round and moved slowly into the exit channel. Two battle flags waved lazily from their halyards high on the ship's masts. A makeshift steel patch on the port bow covered a large hole suffered in the previous battle. Nonetheless, the damaged warship presented a powerful, beautiful picture as she moved gracefully toward her fate."

In the late afternoon of 17 December, Langsdorff headed the battleship back down the estuary towards the British warships. When *Graf Spee* reached a point just beyond the three-mile limit, Captain Langsdorff halted her. The Captain, his officers and crew, then promptly abandoned their ship, leaving in launches. At eight that evening, three time-bombs exploded, ruining the warship and starting a massive fire. *Graf Spee* soon settled in the shallows, scuttled by her crew, her superstructure still above the water. The German merchant ship *Tacoma* rescued some of the crew. For several days the hulk continued to burn.

Again, from Langsdorff of the *Graf Spee, Prince of Honour*: "At 10 a.m. Monday, December 18, two seagoing tugs, *Colaso* and *Gigante*, with the barge *Chiriguana* in tow, approached Buenos Aires. Close to 1,100 weary sailors crowded into every corner of the little ships. Most of the crew wore tropical whites while the officers stood out in their blue uniforms. Men overflowed onto the gunwales and clung to the rigging trying to find breathing space. Exhausted and hungry, their uniforms sweaty and crumpled, the 'shipwrecked' sailors had escaped potential disaster in Montevideo. On the black headbands of their white hats, printed

in Gothic gold letters, blazed the name of their ship—Panzerschiff *Admiral Graf Spee*."

Captain Langsdorff spent the next few days writing letters to his wife and son in Germany and to the German ambassador in Buenos Aires. On the morning of 20 December he shot himself in the head with a pistol borrowed from the German Embassy and was found dead in his room at the Naval Arsenal in Buenos Aires, wrapped in the ensign of his ship. For his actions during this, the first major naval victory for the British in World War Two, Commodore Henry Harwood, commander of British cruiser Force G from HMS *Exeter*, was knighted and promoted to Rear Admiral. British casualties in the battle totalled seventy-two, with sixty-one killed in *Exeter*, seven in *Ajax* and four in *Achilles*. Winston Churchill called the action a great victory which "in a cold and dark winter warmed the cockles of our hearts."

The burnt-out wreck of *Graf Spee* lies in the shallows off Montevideo harbour. Her foretop can still be seen on clear days.

The elderly German battleship *Schleswig-Holstein* entered the Polish harbour of Danzig on what had been billed as a friendly visit in late August of 1939. Six days later, her gun crews opened fire on the Polish fortifications near the harbour. The surprise attack marked the opening shots of the Second World War.

Being in a ship is being in a jail, with the chance of being drowned.
—Samuel Johnson

left: Crewmen of
Graf Spee; below:
The pocket battle-
ship, and, at bottom,
after being scuttled
near Montevideo,
Uruguay in
December 1939.

The German supply ship *Altmark* was sailing through Norwegian waters en route to her home port on 16 February 1940, carrying 299 British prisoners-of-war. They were Merchant Navy and Lascar seamen whose ships had been sunk in the South Atlantic by the pocket battleship *Graf Spee*. The *Altmark* was a 12,000-ton auxiliary warship disguised as a tanker. The British destroyer *Cossack* skippered by Captain Philip Vian, spotted *Altmark* among the fiords and gave chase. *Cossack* caught up with *Altmark* at Jossingfiord near Bergen. It was evening and the crew of the German ship tried to blind the *Cossack* crew with a searchlight. They then charged the British warship astern at full speed, powering through a channel in the ice. *Cossack* skilfully avoided major damage in the encounter. *Altmark* was then boarded by crewmen of *Cossack* who rescued the British sailors. A Lieutenant-Commander Turner led the boarding party and famously shouted to the men he had rescued: "The Navy's here!" The incident caught the imagination of the British public which, at that time, was desperate for any sort of victory. They quickly made Vian a national hero and *Cossack* a household word.

Infamy

The American battleship USS *Arizona*, BB-39, in drydock at Pearl Harbor in 1939.

The expansionist leadership of Japan in December 1941 was proceeding with the plan they called the Great East Asia Co-Existence Sphere, aimed initially at "expanding" their territory into Manchuria and then mainland China. The Japanese armies were actively pursuing these objectives in the 1930s and the Japanese government decided it had to act to secure various strategic commodities that the nation lacked to supply its military needs. The United States government, the President and the Congress, were gravely concerned about the genuine threat posed by Japan's aggressive moves in the Far East and throughout the Pacific, and expressed its view of the Japanese incursions by placing an embargo on Japan that covered steel, scrap iron, aviation spirit and several other potential war materials—this in addition to freezing all Japanese assets in the U.S.

The embargo quickly ramped up the pressure on Japan's leaders who feared for their country's survival without the commodities they required to feed their expansive programme, commodities that included rubber, tin, bauxite and especially the oil of the Dutch East Indies and Malaya, all of which they saw as essential to achieving their goals in China and elsewhere in the Pacific. It was also clear to them that they would have to go to war with the British Empire and with the Dutch government in exile. Too, the extensive military presence of the Americans in the Philippines would almost certainly require war with the United States which was not going to tolerate this sort of adventurism on the part of the Japanese. Thus, the Japanese military planners determined that they would have to destroy the American base facilities in the Philippines, as well as the fleet of the U.S. Navy in Pearl Harbor, Hawaii, as preliminary to taking the East Indies, Malaya, and ultimately, China.

The key personality at the core of planning the Japanese strikes of their Pacific campaign was Harvard-educated Imperial Japanese Navy Admiral Isoroku Yamamoto whose illustrious career had included a stint as a naval attaché in Washington. His experience there had left him with no illusions about American military strength or her quality as an adversary. That knowledge made him oppose war with the U.S., but in the current circumstances he accepted its inevitability. On one occasion in 1940, the admiral addressed a group of Japanese schoolchildren telling them: "Japan cannot defeat America in a war. Therefore, Japan should not fight America." The highly influential Yamamoto warned the people, the military, and the leadership of Japan that, when war came, it would be absolutely essential to "give a fatal blow to the enemy at the outset—when it was least expected. Anything less than the total destruction of the U.S. fleet would awaken a sleeping giant."

The journey to Pearl Harbor for Admiral Yamamoto took him by way of London where, in 1934, he visited with the British historian and naval authority, Hector Bywater who, in 1921, had published the book *Sea Power in the Pacific*. On its publication the book had attracted world-wide interest. In Japan it was soon required reading at the Japanese Naval War College and the Imperial Naval Academy. In it Bywater contended that the Japanese home islands were basically invulnerable to assault by American forces due to the distance to U.S. supply facilities, as well as the secondary fuel and supply consumption required in such an effort. The key to American success in any war against Japan would be, he believed, an island-hopping campaign, through the Marianas to Guam and the Philippines. Then, in 1925, Bywater produced a second book, *The Great Pacific War*, in which he declared that Japan's military success in such a war would hang on her making a devastating surprise attack on the U.S. Navy's

Thanksgiving Day
--MENU--

U.S.S. West Virginia

20 November, 1941

Pearl Harbor TH.

CREAM OF TOMATO SOUP

SALTINES

FRESH SLICED TOMATOES   SWEET PICKLES

ROAST YOUNG TOM TURKEY

GIBLET GRAVY   SAGE STUFFING

CREAMED MASHED POTATOES   GLAZED SWEETS

FRENCH PEAS

HOT SOUTHERN ROLLS   BUTTER

PUMPKIN PIE   ICE CREAM

COFFEE   CIGARETTES

Captain M. S. Bennion, U.S.N.
Commanding Officer.

left: President and Mrs Roosevelt with King George VI and Queen Elizabeth in 1939; above: Japanese Admiral Isoroku Yamamoto; below: The Japanese envoys to the United States in December 1941.

Pacific Fleet, coupled with invasion of Guam and the Philippines. He also declared that Japan would need to effectively fortify her mandate islands.

Admiral Yamamoto met with and had a lengthy conversation with Hector Bywater, having been greatly impressed by his theories and their implications for both Japanese and American strategy. The Bywater theories undoubtedly served to influence the admiral years later when he would conceive, plan and direct the staggering surprise attack on the capital ships and port facilities of the American navy at Pearl Harbor, the raid that took place in the early morning of 7 December 1941.

"Yesterday, December 7th 1941—a date which will live in infamy—the United States of America was suddenly and deliberately attacked by naval and air forces of the Empire of Japan.

"The United States was at peace with that nation, and, at the solicitation of Japan, was still in conversation with its government and its Emperor looking toward the maintenance of peace in the Pacific.

"Indeed, one hour after Japanese air squadrons had commenced bombing in the American island of Oahu, the Japanese Ambassador to the United States and his colleague delivered to our Secretary of State a formal reply to a recent American message. And, while this reply stated that it seemed useless to continue the existing diplomatic negotiations, it contained no threat or hint of war or of armed attack.

"It will be recorded that the distance of Hawaii from Japan makes it obvious that the attack was deliberately planned many days or even weeks ago. During the intervening time the Japanese government has deliberately sought to deceive the United States by false statements and expressions of hope for continued peace.

"The attack yesterday on the Hawaiian Islands has caused severe damage to American naval and military forces. I regret to tell you that very many American lives have been lost. In addition, American ships have been reported torpedoed on the high seas between San Francisco and Honolulu.

"Yesterday the Japanese Government also launched an attack against Malaya. Last night Japanese forces attacked Hong Kong. Last night Japanese forces attacked Guam. Last night Japanese forces attacked the Philippine Islands. Last night the Japanese attacked Wake Island. And this morning the Japanese attacked Midway Island.

"Japan has therefore undertaken a surprise offensive extending throughout the Pacific area. The facts of yesterday and today speak for themselves. The people of the United States have already formed their opinions and well understand the implications to the very life and safety of our nation.

"As Commander-in-Chief of the Army and Navy I have directed that all measures be taken for our defense, that always will our whole nation remember the character of the onslaught against us.

"No matter how long it may take us to overcome this premeditated invasion, the American people, in their righteous might, will win through to absolute victory.

"I believe that I interpret the will of the Congress and of the people when I assert that we will not only defend ourselves to the uttermost but will make it very certain that this form of treachery shall never again endanger us.

above: Pearl Harbor before
the Japanese raid; left: A
Japanese target model used
in their preparation for the
attack on the U.S. fleet.

"Hostilities exist. There is no blinking at the fact that our people, our territory and our interests are in grave danger.

"With confidence in our armed forces, with the unbounding determination of our people, we will gain the inevitable triumph. So help us God.

"I ask that the Congress declare that since the unprovoked and dastardly attack by Japan on Sunday, December 7th 1941, a state of war has existed between the United States and the Japanese Empire."
—President Franklin D. Roosevelt, December 8th, 1941

Nearly thirteen months before the Japanese attack on the American warships and facilities at Pearl Harbor, in the night of 11-12 November 1940, a small force of British Fairey Swordfish bombers and torpedo bombers took part in a raid on the capital ships of the Italian fleet in the southern Italian port of Taranto. Operating from the Royal Navy aircraft carrier HMS *Illustrious*, the planes wrought crippling damage on the enemy vessels, taking about half of them out of action in the exceptionally well-planned and executed attack, for the loss of just two of the British aircraft.

The forethought and planning of the Pearl Harbor attack the following December was undoubtedly influenced to some extent at least by both the theories of historian Hector Bywater, and the methods and results achieved by the British in their raid on the Italian battleships in Taranto harbour. In the spring of 1941, a small party of Imperial Japanese Navy senior officers called upon their Italian counterparts in Taranto. The meeting took place on the deck of the heavily damaged battleship *Littorio*, at the request of the Japanese visitors who were both fascinated and inspired by the British solution to the problem of conducting an effective and successful torpedo attack against capital warships at anchor in a relatively shallow basin, a harbour characteristic common to both Taranto and Pearl.

Prior to the Taranto attack, the anchorages of both the Italian port and Pearl had been thought proper and safe by their resident fleet commanders. Both harbours adjoined cities which, in 1940, had populations of about 200,000. Both were well defended and posed a significant threat to any enemy force. With their interests in Egypt, India, Singapore, and Gibraltar in mind, the British felt substantially threatened by the presence of the Italian fleet at Taranto; the Japanese saw the U.S. Navy presence in Pearl Harbor as a definite impediment to their expansionist programme in Southeast Asia.

The challenges to the British Swordfish planes flying to Taranto included how to approach the target area from the Mediterranean without being spotted by Italian reconnaissance aircraft; how to evade the anti-aircraft fire of fifty-four enemy warships and twenty-one shore batteries; how to avoid the steel cables of more than fifty barrage balloons; and how to avoid the attentions of squadrons of Italian fighter planes; and perhaps the greatest challenge of all—how to successfully deliver torpedoes by aircraft onto the target vessels in the shallow basin.

In his planning of the Pearl raid, Admiral Yamamoto required a thirty-two ship task force assembled around six great aircraft carriers, *Akagi, Hiryu, Kaga, Shokaku, Soryu,* and *Zuikaku.* This large force would need to sail—undetected—roughly 4,000 miles from Japan to a point within 200 miles of Pearl target. From that point, his carrier aircraft, which would be almost at the limit of their range, would be required to approach and cope with the defensive fire

of up to sixty-eight warships, the enemy shore batteries, and at least 100 enemy fighter planes.

Adjoining the site of the present Honolulu airport, the shallow harbour at Pearl surrounds the small airfield facility of Ford Island. The harbour has a single narrow channel to the ocean. On its eastern end lay dry docks, a submarine base, and, crucially, an oil storage tank farm. On the morning of the Japanese raid, seven battleships of the American Pacific fleet lay at anchor in the harbour southeast of Ford Island; USS *Arizona*, USS *California*, USS *Maryland*, USS *Nevada*, USS *Oklahoma*, USS *Tennessee*, and USS *West Virginia*. The USS *Pennsylvania* lay in a nearby dry dock undergoing a refit. Yamamoto knew too that not all the capital ships of the U.S. Navy's Pacific Fleet would be in Pearl Harbor on the day of the attack; some were home-ported on the American west coast, some were in refit, and some might be in transit between the west coast and Hawaii or elsewhere at sea. In late 1941, just two American aircraft carriers were operational in the Pacific, *Enterprise* and *Lexington*. A third carrier, *Saratoga*, was in the Bremerton, Washington navy yard for a major refit. The Japanese admiral accepted the fact that he would have to mount a vital second strike attack on what remained of the U.S. Pacific fleet within six months of the Pearl strike. The key to the success of the Japanese attack lay with the delivery of the torpedoes. Torpedo technology (prior to the

top left: An American casualty of the Pearl Harbor raid; top right: The explosion that tore apart the battleship *Arizona*; far left: A massive oil fire shrouds the battleship USS *California* following the Japanese attack; below: The battleship USS *Nevada* afire after the attack by hundreds of carrier-based Japanese fighters, bombers, and torpedo planes on Sunday, 7 December 1941.

to the Taranto raid) meant that the missile would normally sink to a depth of at least seventy feet before it would level off and head to its target. Such a weapon would certainly become mired in the muddy bed of basins like Taranto and Pearl, so, following the IJN May 1941 visit to the Italian port, the munitions engineers of the Mitsubishi company near Nagasaki were ordered to design and develop a new torpedo which would incorporate a special stabilizing fin. Dropped correctly, the new weapon would sink to less than the forty-foot depth of the Pearl basin and proceed unimpeded to its target vessel. 180 of the new torpedoes had been delivered to the IJN aircraft carriers by mid-November.

By the autumn of 1939, President Roosevelt, with an eye on Japan's aggressive stance in the Far East, had decided to reposition the bulk of the U.S. Pacific fleet from its base in San Diego to a new home port in Pearl Harbor, Hawaii. The president knew that his navy was not yet at sufficient strength for major offensive operations, and that his defenses at Pearl Harbor were not yet completed, but he wanted to send a powerful, unequivocal message to the Japanese leadership.

Far from trembling at the prospect of a major confrontation with the Americans, when the Japanese planners learned of the U.S. Pacific fleet relocation to Pearl, they were highly motivated by the successes of their German allies in the Blitzkrieg actions across western Europe, and by their own intense interest in invading the British, French, and Dutch colonies in Asia.

The U.S. Ambassador to Japan in the 1930s, Joseph Grew, was thoroughly versed in the ways of the Japanese and the militant Japanese government, and by the middle of the decade was warning Roosevelt and the U.S. government of Japan's aggressive posture towards all of East Asia: "There is a swashbuckling temper in the country . . . that might lead the government to any extremes and eventually to national suicide." The U.S. Congress and the American people then were overwhelmingly isolationist, and Roosevelt was somewhat limited in his ability to respond to Japan. By late in the decade, however, American attitudes toward Japan were changing and with that in mind, the president asked Congress for a substantial increase in naval appropriations, to expand America's two-ocean navy. He followed that act by establishing what he referred to as a "moral embargo", a request to U.S. munitions and aircraft manufacturers not to sell their products to Japan. The request proved quite effective. Ambassador Grew, meanwhile, now warned Roosevelt that the Japanese government saw the present climate as "a golden opportunity to pursue their expansionist desires unhampered by the allegedly hamstrung democracies. The German military machine and system, and their brilliant successes, have gone to the Japanese head like strong wine."

A new ruling cabinet was in place in Japan and it was dominated by two especially formidable personalities, Minister of War Lieutenant General Hideki Tojo and Foreign Minister Yosuke Matsuoka. Matsuoka grew up and was educated in Portland, Oregon, and thought himself something of an authority on America. Such was his influence in the cabinet that he was given considerable latitude in the development of Japanese foreign policy, much more than any previous foreign minister had been permitted. He was perceived as brilliant, but somewhat arrogant and inclined to be erratic, and was prone to curry favour with his American counterpart, Secretary of State Cordell Hull. He was also known to have told an American newspaper correspondent that democracy was finished; that fascism would prevail in the coming

top: American aircraft and hangars burning on Ford Island in Pearl after the raid; above; Another victim of the attack, his car riddled by machine-gun bullets.

war, and that there wasn't room enough in the world for two systems of government. Secretary Hull had no illusions about the current Japanese government or its motives. He was quite sure they were leading to war between Japan and the United States.

Hull had a significant advantage over Matsuoka. In August 1940, Japan's primary diplomatic code was deciphered by American cryptographers who were intercepting and then reading the secret cable traffic moving between Tokyo and the Japanese foreign embassies. Hull referred to the intercepts by the code name Magic and he was in the enviable position of knowing the truth behind every seemingly sincere peace offering extended by Admiral Kichisaburo Nomura, the Japanese special envoy to Washington, sent there ostensibly to resolve the differences between Japan and the U.S., by diplomatic means. U.S., by diplomatic means. Having already read the Magic intercepts on each occasion, Hull knew that the Japanese were, in fact, preparing for war rather than pursuing peace. He hated their duplicity and underhandedness, despising their methods.

The capsized battleship USS *Oklahoma* in the foreground with the USS *Maryland* behind her, following the raid.

In moves that further infuriated Hull, Matsuoka soon made an alliance with the fascist governments of Germany and Italy, as well as applying pressure on the French Vichy government for permission to base Japanese troops in French Indochina (now Vietnam), which President Roosevelt, Prime Minister Winston Churchill, and Cordell Hull perceived as preparation to invade Malaya, Burma, or possibly Singapore. When the Vichy granted that permission, Japanese aircraft and soldiers were moved into Indochina in large numbers. It was no surprise to Roosevelt and Hull who knew all about it from the Magic intercepts.

Now, in addition to the other items and commodities embargoed against Japan, Roosevelt announced a total embargo on all oil shipments to the Japanese, a further warning to halt their war policy in China and East Asia. For their part, the Japanese stepped up their "peace offensive" by sending diplomatic reinforcements to assist Nomura in Washington. Roosevelt and Hull underscored their opposition to Japan's militant policies, telling the Japanese government that the oil embargo would remain in place until they got out of China and Indochina, and renounced their Tri-partite agreement with Germany and Italy. In response, the Japanese refused to comply and made a demand of their own, that the U.S. cease providing arms to the Chinese Nationalist leader, Chiang Kai-Shek. Ambassador Grew, at that point, was trying to persuade President Roosevelt not to make the Japanese government feel that it was cornered; he believed they would then be compelled to violent reaction. Grew saw what he felt might be an opportunity in August, when the Japanese foreign minister was replaced by the more reasoned Admiral Teijiro Toyoda, whom Grew knew and understood. With the accession of Toyoda, Grew urged his boss, Secretary Hull, and the president to use "constructive conciliation" rather than "economic strangulation" in their relations with Japan.

Roosevelt and Hull were not receptive to Grew's recommendations. They knew, from the Magic intercepts, that the Japanese had plans for conquest throughout Asia, and the president was under considerable pressure from the Chinese Nationalists to both increase the arms and financial assistance being provided to them, and to take a hard, unyielding position against Japan, a position strongly supported by Roosevelt's Navy and War Secretaries, Frank Knox and Henry Stimson, respectively. Both men believed that Japan was bluffing, would probably be unwilling to fight if it came to that, and was not militarily powerful enough to be a great threat if war with the U.S. did result. Winston Churchill tried to influence Roosevelt along those same lines. The president, however, had been briefed by his army and navy chiefs that the U.S. armed forces were not yet ready to fight a war, and he persisted with efforts to achieve some sort of accord with the Japanese.

By autumn, the Japanese envoys in Washington were offering that Japan would halt her military activity in Southeast Asia and, upon the restoration of peace in China and the Pacific region, would withdraw her troops from all foreign soil, in exchange for a resumption of oil shipments. President Roosevelt countered with a proposal that the U.S. would resume economic relations with Japan if Japan would stop her military moves to the north and south and renew peace negotiations with China. That idea never went to Japan, however, as Cordell Hull learned that right then a Japanese task force of warships and troops was steaming through the China Sea towards Southeast Asia and possibly the Dutch East Indies. Instead of the president's counter-proposal, Hull delivered a ten-point document demanding that Japan withdraw from China, Indochina, and Manchuria; and renounce their Tri-partite agreement with Germany and Italy. Hull's document served to validate Ambassador Grew's perspective.

It seemed to convince the Japanese of American intransigence and the hopelessness of any further negotiation with the U.S.

The Japanese envoy in Washington, Mr Nomura, requested an appointment on 7 December to see Secretary Hull at 1 p.m. that day. He later telephoned to ask that the appointment be changed to 1:45 p.m. as he was not quite ready for the meeting. He arrived at 2:05 and was received by Hull at 2:20. He told Hull that he had been instructed to deliver a document at 1 p.m., and handed it to the Secretary. Nomura apologized for the delay saying he had needed more time to decode the message. When Hull asked him why he had specified a one o'clock meeting, he said he didn't know. Hull read the first few pages of the

U.S. Navy efforts to right the capsized battleship USS *Oklahoma* were unsuccessful until 1943.

document and asked Nomura if it was being presented under the instructions of the Japanese Government. Nomura said it was, and when Hull finished reading it, he said, "I must say that in all my conversations with you during the last nine months, I have never uttered one word of untruth. The is borne out absolutely by the record. In all my fifty years of public service I have never seen a document that was more crowded with infamous falsehoods and distortions—infamous falsehoods and distortions on a scale so huge that I never imagined until today that any government on this planet was capable of uttering them." Nomura left the room without comment.

Admiral Yamamoto presented his completed plan for the Japanese attack on the U.S. Navy in Pearl Harbor, to the Imperial Navy General Staff which totally and absolutely opposed it. They said that the essential element of surprise would be impossible to preserve, with an armada of six large carriers and more than twenty support vessels sailing half-way across the Pacific. They said that the only route that would avoid possible encounters with commercial shipping traffic was across the north Pacific, which would make refueling far more difficult in the frequently stormy seas up there. They pointed out too, that, should the attack have to be aborted for some reason, the Japanese fleet might have to fight the American fleet in unfamiliar waters. Finally, they collectively challenged that the inherent risks in the plan far outweighed the potential gains. The admiral countered their arguments and followed by threatening to resign his commission and retire if his plan was not approved. It was.

Preparations for the raid on Pearl advanced through November as the latest information on U.S. Navy fleet movements, berthing positions in the harbour, and duty schedules were cabled to Yamamoto's headquarters by the Japanese Consul General in Honolulu. On 25 November, the assembled carrier task force sailed east from Hitokappu Bay in the Kurile Islands north of Japan. The ships travelled in strict radio silence across the western Pacific. Per the admiral's plan, with precise coordination, other Japanese striking forces reached their destinations at about the same time as the main Pearl strike force arrived at its launch point a few hundred miles north of Oahu Island, Hawaii, where the dawn was just breaking.

Vice Admiral Chiuchi Nagumo, commander of the Japanese naval task force heading for Hawaii, received a coded signal from Admiral Yamamoto on 2 December authorizing him to proceed with the attack; it read Niitaka Yama Nabora—Climb Mount Niitaka. By 6 a.m. the first wave of dive-bombers, horizontal bombers, fighters and torpedo bombers had launched and was assembling. At 7:53 a.m. the 183 aircraft rounded Barber's Point southwest of Pearl and flight leader Lieutenant Commander Mitsuo Fuchida used the code phrase Tora! Tora! Tora! (Tiger! Tiger! Tiger!) to alert the carrier task force that the aircraft were about to commence the attack. First to descend from the formation were the torpedo bombers positioning to make their low-level drops. Their initial targets were a minelayer, a light cruiser, and the battleship *Arizona*. The torpedo that struck *Arizona* literally blew her out of the water, ripping her bottom out. Then the battleships *California* and *Oklahoma* received massive damage when each was hit by three torpedoes. Within a few moments, *Oklahoma* was struck by a fourth torpedo, which caused her to capsize. As the horizontal bombers opened their attack, one of their bombs exploded in the forward magazine of *Arizona*, blowing the ship apart and bringing the loss of more than 1,000 of her crew members. The attacks on the battleships

above: The USS *California* has settled on the harbour bottom in this photo taken the day after the surprise attack; left: The hull of the *Oklahoma* after she was finally refloated on 8 March 1943.

below: January 1944, the U.S. battleship *Alabama*, centre, in Pearl Harbor, with the aircraft carrier *Enterprise* in the background.; at bottom: The Ford Island mooring point of the battleship, USS *West Virginia*.

and facilities in Pearl continued savagely, while in other parts of the island, at Hickam and Wheeler airfields, and at the Kaneohe Bay Naval Air Station, other planes from the first wave formation bombed and strafed the many parked American aircraft. Fighters dropped to strafe U.S. Marines as they ran from their barracks. Exactly one hour after the arrival of the first wave of Japanese aircraft over the island, the planes of the second wave roared in over Pearl to continue the strike.

Of the eight American battleships in Pearl Harbor that December Sunday morning, two, *Oklahoma* and *Arizona*, were damaged beyond repair. Of the others, *California*, *Nevada*, and *West Virginia* were all extensively damaged and put out of action. *Maryland*, *Tennessee*, and *Pennsylvania* suffered major damage, and three light cruisers were badly damaged, while three destroyers were sunk. 164 American aircraft were destroyed on the ground at the two airfields and on Ford Island; 159 more were damaged. 2,395 servicemen and civilians were killed in the raid and a further 1,178 were wounded. Twenty-nine of the Japanese aircraft were lost in the attack, some as the result of accidents. The six Japanese aircraft carriers went undetected.

Richard McCutcheon was a powder car man, running an electric hoist back and forth down to the upper handling room of the battleship USS *West Virginia*: "There was nothing but powder in that room. It was directly under the projectile room where the shells were kept. We all trained so that we knew every job around the turret. I always wanted to be a gunner's mate, so I asked around to find out how I could get re-assigned and was told to see a turret captain. I went to see him and he had to check with the division officer and they took me in the turret and put me to work on the number two gun. Each man there had a part of the inside of the turret he had to take care of and wipe down and clean and shine every day.

"On December 6th, a lot of us were out sunning ourselves on the upper deck, until it got so hot that you had to run down and jump in the showers. A typical Saturday in Pearl. It was good duty. On Sunday mornings we had breakfast and I had the duty. My station was to handle a fire extinguisher. That day a third of the ship's company had liberty on shore. The bugle sounded 'Fire and Rescue' and I ran off to get my white hat from my locker. The Officer of the Deck at this point thought that there had been some kind of explosion over the Ten-Ten dock. A torpedo had passed under a ship there and hit a cruiser and they both sank. And then we were ordered to General Quarters.

"Then I realized it was the Japs. I started running aft. I went up two decks heading to the turret. On the way I saw a plane and wondered what he was doing. He turned and went toward the *California* and as he turned I saw the red ball on the wing. Before I got to the turret there was a tremendous shaking and, by then the ladder was full. I went around to another ladder and got up to the top deck. From there I went up to the boat deck and under the overhang of the turret to my battle station in the turret.

"The explosions continued ; the ship would shake and the blast covers would clang, and then we started listing slowly to port, very slowly, and I was watching that and thinking that we might have to get through that hatch door in the bottom of the turret pretty soon. Meanwhile, the damage control officer managed to counter-flood to keep the ship from capsizing. She eventually just settled to the bottom.

U.S. President Franklin Roosevelt
signing the American declaration of
war on 8 December 1941.

"The hatch cover was still open and someone stuck his head up and yelled 'Abandon ship!' 'Abandon ship!' We got out and there was no big rush. The Tennessee was inboard of us and we made it to the fo'c'sle, took our shoes off and jumped into the water and swam to Ford Island. When we got to shore the first thing we heard was 'Get down! Get down! Strafing!' I got down by a truck at the edge of the golf course as a plane turned toward us and began firing. The tracers seemed to be coming right at me. Only one of his guns was firing. I got under the truck and the tracers turned away from me. About then a woman came down from one of the houses there, carrying clothes. I wandered over to see what was going on and she fitted us out with dry clothes."

On Sundays the sailors of the USS *Arizona* breakfasted on beans, cornbread and coffee. The Navy allotment for food since the 1920s was forty cents per man per day.

Ted Mason, USS *California*: "Properly buttoned up, the *California* could have shrugged off two or even three torpedoes, with minor listing that would have been quickly corrected by counter-flooding the starboard voids. Instead she had assumed a port list of fourteen or fifteen degrees and the list was still increasing. Suddenly I found myself sliding toward the low side of the 'birdbath', which brought me up sharply against the splinter shield. My earphones were jerked from my head. Before replacing them, I looked down. A hundred feet below me was nothing but dirty, oil-streaked and flotsam-filled water. Lifeless bodies from the *Oklahoma* floated face down. Motor launches were criss-crossing the channel, picking up swimming sailors.

"If the *California* capsized—and that I could see was a distinct possibility—I had at least a fighting chance to join the swimmers. My shipmates below decks had none.

"I planned to climb to the opposite side of the splinter shield as the ship went over and launch myself in a long, flat dive when the maintop touched the water. If I could avoid getting fouled in the yardarm rigging or the radio antennas, I just might get clear.

"Ahead of the *Nevada*, a large pipeline snaked out from Ford Island in a semicircle ending at the dredge *Turbine*. Since it blocked more than half the channel, the line was always disconnected and pulled clear when the battleships were scheduled to stand out. This morning, of course, it was still in place. But the sailor conning the *Nevada* squeezed her between the dredge and the dry dock area without slowing down.

"The flames were now shooting up past her anti-aircraft detectors nearly to her foretop. She had been hit repeatedly and Pearl Harbor was pouring into her hull. Her bow was low in the water. If she were to sink in the channel, she would plug up the entire harbour like a cork in a bottle. With bitter regret, we watched her run her bow into shallow water between the floating dry dock and Hospital Point. The current carried her stern around, and she finished her evolution pointing back up the channel she had tried so valiantly to follow to freedom."

At the height of his business career Kazuo Sakamaki became the head of Toyota's Brazilian operations. In December 1941, Sakamaki was a twenty-three-year-old ensign in the Imperial Japanese Navy and one-half of the crew of a midget submarine struggling to enter Pearl Harbor. His mission was to sneak into the port unobserved, ahead of the main attack by the carrier aircraft, and be ready to sink one of the target battleships at the appropriate moment.

It was a suicide mission involving five such midget subs. But the gyrocompass of Sakamaki's boat failed and the other four subs were either lost of destroyed during the attack.

Sakamaki's boat became stranded on a coral reef down the coast and he was forced to abandon it. He was later discovered, unconscious, by an American soldier, and became the first Japanese prisoner-of-war in World War Two. He recalled feeling deep shame with the failure of his mission, for letting his sub fall into enemy hands, and for surviving when his comrades had died in the attempted raid. In time though, he gradually overcame the guilt he felt and went on to help his fellow Japanese prisoners in POW camps in the United States.

Where were America's aircraft carriers, important warships that would become her new capital ships in the Second World War, on Sunday 7 December 1941? The USS *Lexington* had departed Pearl Harbor on 5 December in order to supplement the air defenses of Midway Island. While en route the *Lexington* commander was notified of the attack on Pearl. He launched search planes to look for the Japanese fleet and then joined with two other U.S. Navy task forces to search southwest of Hawaii, returning to Pearl on 13 December. The USS *Saratoga*, sister ship of the *Lexington*, was entering San Diego bay, having recently emerged from a dry dock at Bremerton, Washington, where she had undergone a refit. The USS *Ranger*, the first U.S. Navy ship to be designed and built from the keel up as an aircraft carrier, was returning to her port, Norfolk, Virginia, from a patrol in the Caribbean at the time of the attack. The USS *Yorktown* was at her home port, Norfolk, on 7 December. The USS *Enterprise* had left Pearl Harbor on 28 November to deliver twelve Grumman F4F-3 Wildcat fighters to a Marine fighter squadron on Wake Island. She was returning to Pearl when it was attacked. Several of her aircraft were launched and eighteen of them arrived over Pearl while the attack was still under way. Six planes from *Enterprise* were lost in the action. The USS *Wasp* was at anchor in Grassy Bay, Bermuda, on the 7th. The USS *Hornet* was conducting a training cruise in the Atlantic on the day of the attack. The USS *Long Island*, a smaller escort-type carrier, was in Norfolk that day. Five other U.S. Navy carriers were in various stages of construction on the day Pearl Harbor was attacked. They were the USS *Essex*, USS *Bon Homme Richard*, USS *Intrepid*, USS *Cabot*, and the USS *Bunker Hill*. No U.S. Navy carriers were in Pearl Harbor on the day of the Japanese attack, a fact that would haunt Japan's war planners, especially Admiral Yamamoto.

In the late afternoon, several hours after the last enemy raider had flown from Pearl Harbor, two young American naval officers went over to the wreck of the USS *Arizona* in a motor launch. As the sun began to set they carefully retrieved the American flag that had furled from the stern of the battleship, but was partially submerged in the oily water of the harbour. Other navy personnel visited the remains of the American warships. They brought mattress covers in which to hold the bodies and body parts they found as they explored the ruined hulks. While they worked, mass graves 150 feet long, just trenches really, were being bulldozed on Oahu to hold the hundreds of roughly-fashioned wooden boxes, some of which were leaking oil or blood. Confusion dominated America's towns and cities that day. People across the country, including the president, his cabinet, and the members of Congress, were anxious, perplexed, angry, and looking for answers. By late afternoon in Washington, Japan had formally declared war on the United States and the British Empire. The Japanese emperor stated: "Japan, for its existence and self-defense, has no other recourse but to appeal to arms and to crush every obstacle in its path".

below: A sixteen-inch shell on the deck of the USS *Missouri* in Pearl Harbor. "I had the honor to be the last battleship captain in the world, and that was while in command of the USS *Missouri*. I was CO when she was recommissioned on 10 May 1986 and when she was decomissioned on 31 March 1993. She served the United States in three wars and always did her job in the highest professional manner. If you were to ask me what made her great, there is only one answer in my opinion . . . and that is HER CREW. From 1944 to 1992, they were always equal to the task and true professionals. I always believed they stood six inches taller than any other sailors in the fleet. That is the story of the 'Mighty Mo', the last of the great ships."
—Albert Lee Kaiss, Captain, USN Ret.

According to Mike Holloman, a powder hoist operator for the sixteen-inch fifty-calibre centre gun of turret number three on the USS *Missouri* in 1985: "It really isn't terribly noisy inside the gun room during firing, but the feeling and excitement are something else. The big guns are always fired off the side of the ship; shooting straight along the beam is too hard on her. The ship acts as a part of the recoil. You feel her sway from top to bottom after firing a broadside, then she settles out. Some say that firing a broadside pushes the ship back about thirty feet, but this is debateable. When the guns are fired, there is a faint smell of rotten eggs, from the black powder primer charge.

"From the gun room level, down to the ammunition magazines, it takes about seventy men to operate one of the sixteen-inch gun turrets on an *Iowa* class battleship. A really good crew can shoot two rounds per minute per gun. The range is a little over twenty miles."

There are three guns in each of the three big gun turrets of an *Iowa* class battleship. Each of the turrets weighs 160 tons. Holloman: "Each gun has its own powder hoist which brings up 660 pounds of powder per shot, in six 110-pound bags. The bags are made of silk so they will completely burn away on ignition and they contain about 480 grains of smokeless-powder charge. The powder bags are subject to detonation under shock, because of a black-powder ignition pad (identified by the red-coloured end of the bag) quilted to the back of each bag to ensure instant ignition on firing. Once, while moving powder cans on the overhead rail system down in the magazines (each can contained three of the 110-pound bags), a can suddenly dropped about two feet to the deck. We all froze and then looked up to see that a section of the railing was missing. The event caused a lot of hearts to beat faster.

"The gun room itself has five men working in it. They are: Gun Captain, who is in charge of the gun, the powder hoist operator; the projectile operator, who also works the rammer; the primer man, who cleans the primer hole and puts the primer in; and the powderman, who helps handle the powder.

"All varieties of the projectiles weigh 2,700 pounds, except the armour-piercing type, which weighs 1,900 pounds. When a projectile comes up from the projectile deck, it is rammed into the breech, or chamber section of the gun, while the gun is primed. Next come three powder bags which are rammed into the breech after the projectile. Three more powder bags are placed in the loading tray and a foil pack to reduce fouling, is inserted between the fifth and sixth bags. The remaining powder bags are pushed gently into the breech to avoid setting off the black-powder base. The last bag to go in is positioned next to the breech plug. The primer man then puts a primer the size of a shotgun shell into the firing lock of the breech. The breech is then closed and the gun goes into 'battery' and is ready to shoot. Everyone in the gun room must pay careful attention to where they are standing, especially the primer man. Just before the gun is fired, three tones are sounded. It fires on the third tone.

"After the initial firing of a big gun, it returns to the loading position. Before the breech is opened, a 16psi blast of air is manually sent through the barrel to clear out any burning embers. After the first shot is fired, the gun clears the barrel on its own. Once the breech has been opened, the face is wiped by the Gun Captain to clean it and ensure that no burning powder remains on it which could ignite the next powder bags prior to re-closing the breech."

Tony Alessandro, another powder hoist operator on *Missouri* (1944-1945): "By the time we shot the guns it was automatic because we had practiced so much. When you fire for real, it's like starting a football game; you just get ready to receive the kick-off. The firing became routine, except when we went to the Japanese home islands. Off Honshu, we didn't know what to expect. We didn't want to be like a duck in a shooting gallery."

Herb Fahr was a member of the *Missouri* crew in 1954: "The only gunnery practice I had seen was with the five-inch and the 40 millimeters. I wasn't prepared for the shock that goes through the ship when those sixteen-inch guns go off. We could feel it in the bowels of the ship, like thunder in a cave. The barbershop was the only place in the ship that had four-foot flourescent lights, and when the sixteen-inch guns were going to be fired, those flourescent tubes had to be removed or they would have shattered.

"I wanted to see those guns go off, so I got permission. The best place to observe was up on the 07 or 08 decks where the lookout and gun trainers were. What a sight that was! A broadside brought a flash of fire and smoke a hundred yards out, and the sound was incredibly loud. The water adjacent to the ship would get foamed-up from the concussion and the sideways motion of the ship from the recoil. Watching those guns go off was one of the most thrilling moments of my life."

The big guns of the *Iowa* class battleship represent the ultimate refinement of a weapon, the naval gun, which was first deployed some 600 years ago when the English king, Edward III, known as the 'King of the Sea', had a few guns fitted to some of his ships prior to the Hundred

The battleship USS *Iowa* shelling an enemy position while off the Korean coast in 1950.

Years' War. The first use of 'big guns' in battle at sea was at the battle of Sluys in 1340, though little resulted from employment of the guns. The British prevailed over their French enemy thanks to the superiority of their archers. But this trial spawned the beginnings of naval gun power. By the end of the sixteenth century. A wide range of naval gun types had been fitted into a variety of ships.

While there is disagreement among historians about the origins of gunpowder, the consensus favours China. Early Chinese literature tells of ninth-century Thang alchemists who, while trying to develop the 'elixir of immortality', accidentally invented what they referred to as 'fire drug' or 'fire chemical'. The earliest known reference to the composition of gunpowder was made in 1004, but no specific formula was provided.

By the eleventh century, the Chinese had had considerable experience using gunpowder in fireworks and they employed that background to develop the world's first bombs and grenades. Their interest in the potential military uses of gunpowder led them to strictly control their production of saltpetre amd sulphur and to strictly ban the sale of these ingredients to foreigners. Just how the knowledge of gunpowder and its composition was acquired by Westerners is not known, but by the mid-fourteenth century the first guns had appeared on the battlefields of Europe.

In 1625, the difficulty of producing saltpetre in Europe caused King Charles I of England to publish the following order: "Loving subjects . . . inhabiting within every city, town and village . . . shall carefully and constantly keep and preserve all the urine of man during the whole year, and all the stale of beasts which they can save and gather together whilst their beasts are in their stables and stalls, and that they be careful to use the best means of gathering together and preserving the urine and stale, without mixture of water or thing put therein. Which our commandment and royal pleasure being easy to observe, and so necessary for the public service of us and our people, that if any person do be remiss hereof we shall esteem all such persons contemptuous and ill affected both to our person and estate, and are resolved to proceed to the punishment of that offender with what severity we may."

In their defeat of the Spanish Armada in the English Channel in August 1588, the English navy had elected to engage the enemy at a great range rather than at close quarters. It was the advent of the new era in naval warfare. But the naval gun battles of that time generally yielded more sound and fury than actual damage. In those days, naval guns were clumsy and troublesome weapons, requiring much time and effort in loading, and they had to be retracted from their firing positions to be reloaded. Gunpowder at that time was expensive and, at sea, was subject to dampness. Quality control in its manufacture was uneven at best, and when the weapons were fired, the limited spaces of the gundecks were shrouded in filthy black smoke. There was little precision in the manufacture of cannon, making them unreliable and greatly limiting their accuracy and effectiveness in damaging enemy vessels.

The eighteenth-century HMS *Victory*, among the most famous of all warships, brought a formidable striking power into battle. An excellent description of the firing preparation for the big cannon of the English warship is provided on the HMS *Victory* website: "The Royal Navy trained hard and well [in the days of Admiral Nelson] and could reload the thirty-two-pounder cannon in ninety seconds. This was quite a remarkable time, given the considerable

The bridge and superstructure of the Japanese battleship *Nagato* while under inspection by American naval personnel in August 1945.

Crewmen of the USS *Missouri* are stripping paint from the sixteen-inch main guns while their ship returns to the west coast of the United States.

THE·WONDER·BOOK·OF
THE·NAVY

amount of manhandling required to move the 3.5 tonne gun backwards and forwards, and far shorter than that achieved by French or Spanish crews. It is little wonder that the most common injury to gun crews was abdominal rupture.

"When the gun was fired it recoiled inboard, restrained by the large ropes attached to the rear of the gun barrel. A sponge was dipped in water and thrust down the barrel to remove any traces of burning powder. The new charge and wad were then inserted into the barrel and rammed hard against the rear of the gun. The wad held the charge in place and ensured that the powder was tightly compressed. Next, the rammer was removed and the ball inserted, held in place by a further wad rammed hard down the barrel. A pricker was inserted into the breech hole to open the gunpowder charge and then a small quantitiy of fine powder was poured down the firing hole and into the flint lock pan. The flint lock was cocked and the gun was ready to fire.

"The gun was served by a six-man crew, known by numbers to make orders easier in the noise of battle. Number One was the Gun Captain, who aimed and fired the gun; Number Two used a long spike to turn and raise the barrel; Number Three loaded the gun and rammed the shot and powder home; Number Four sponged out the gun, ensuring that no burning powder or waste was left to cause premature ignition of the new charge; Number Five worked opposite Number Two, to move the gun, whilst Number Six was the smallest and youngest member of the crew—the powder monkey. Often a young boy, perhaps only ten or twelve years old, the powder monkey collected the gunpowder charges from them magazine deep in the hold of the ship and carried them to the gun.

"The whole 3.5 tonnes was now run out, with the crew straining on the carriage ropes to pull the gun muzzle through the gun port in the side of the ship. When the gun came to bear on the target, the Gun Captain pulled the lanyard to the flint lock. As the flint scraped across the pan, a shower of sparks ignited the fine powder, which ignited the main charge and the gun fired, ejecting its iron ball with a forward velocity of some 500 metres per second. The gun would recoil backwards at some two metres per second, and the process of cleaning and reloading began again.

"The gun could be loaded with a variety of shot—from the plain cannon ball to bar shot, chain shot and grape shot. Bar and chain shot whirled around in flight and was intended to cut through enemy rigging, bringing down masts, sails and spars and disabling the ship. Grape shot was an anti-personnel weapon, firing a quantity of smaller balls in a cluster. These spread out and created a murderous hail of metal across an enemy deck. The thirty-two-pound cannon ball was effective in punching through the wooden walls of the enemy, creating a huge spray of deadly flying splinters. At close range, the thirty-two-pound ball was capable of penetrating wood to a depth of several feet.

"With the enemy holed and disabled and the crew killed or wounded with grape shot, the attacking ship could now close the enemy and board the vessel to secure victory. Boarding with close-quarter hand-to-hand fighting was often the deciding factor in battle."

As the battleship was gradually transformed from a wind-powered wooden vessel to a steam-driven ship of steel, her weaponry was greatly improved, and so was her armour, to counter the effects of the improved weaponry of the enemy. The great naval powers were all determined to build high-speed battleships with powerful armament and theoretically in-

above: Lowering a sixteen-inch gun into a turret of the USS *North Carolina* during her fitting-out.

vulnerable protective armour. But attempting to combine these qualities inevitably resulted in a conflict. Protection could only be achieved at the expense of speed, and vice versa; the heavier the guns, the less the protection and/or the speed. Naval armour is heavy and the amount of it needed to provide proper protection for a giant warship was immense. Coping with the threats of heavy shells, mines, torpedoes and, ultimately, aerial bombs, was a supreme challenge for naval architects. The whole ship could not possibly be clad in armour of uniform thickness; instead the armour had to be concentrated where it was most needed, in horizontal armour belts that protected the engine and boiler rooms, and the magazines, from torpedoes and shell fire, and on the turrets which housed the ship's main armament. The thickness of this protective belt increased over the years in response to the improving armour-piercing capability of big naval guns; the most extreme example being the 1881 masted turret ship *Inflexible*, with her compound iron armour which varied from sixteen to twenty-four inches in thickness. No thicker armour has ever been employed in a battleship.

The advances in metallurgy that had made improved ship armour possible had also led to development of the armour-piercing shell, which in turn led to a further evolution in protective armour. Improved steel-making techniques had resulted in metals of extraordinary hardness and strength.

It was not until late in the nineteenth century that the major problems with naval guns were finally resolved. By the 1820s, Russian warships were mounting guns that could fire explosive shells as well as grape shot and case shot. In the 1850s, gun-barrel rifling—spiral grooving which caused the projectile to spin as it was fired (for greater accuracy)—was in use and breech loading was beginning to replace muzzle loading, significantly improving a gun's rate of fire. Spring or hydraulic recoil mechanisms were replacing ropes and crude, slow-burning fuses were replaced, initially by clockwork devices and later by percussion and concussion fuses. Near the end of the century, forged steel shells were developed—the first shells capable of striking and penetrating armour without disintegrating. The projectile had evolved from a sphere to a cylindrical shape and, by the 1890s, its explosive ingredients had changed from gunpowder as both propellant and filler, to cordite and other smokeless powders for the propellant and nitroglycerine compounds for the filler. Muzzle velocity, or the speed at which a shell leaves the gun barrel, was increased with the development of new explosive propellants and the range of shells was improved as the big gun barrels were lengthened and, increasingly, rifled.

Methods for sighting the big guns were crude and relatively ineffective until the introduction of the optical rangefinder near the end of the nineteenth century, to aid in locating the target and calculating its distance from the ship. These rangefinders would eventually reach nearly fifty feet in length and were mounted on the highest part of the battleship superstructure, where the equipment could function to optimum capability. This capability, together with advances in the predictors which allowed a gun to be kept on target despite the speed and roll of the ship, and the possible movement of the target during the time it took for the shell to reach it, dramatically improved the effectiveness of battleship big guns.

Big naval guns reached their ultimate evolution with the design and construction of the largest and most powerful warship ever built, Japan's *Yamato*. The eighteen-inch main guns of *Yamato* and her sister ship *Musashi* were capable of sending shells to a maximum range of

The listing, heavily-damaged Japanese battleship *Ise* in August 1945, with details and camouflage of her bridge superstructure clearly defined. Following their loss of four aircraft carriers at Midway in June 1942, the Japanese began converting *Ise* and her sister ship *Hyuga*, to hybrid battleship-carriers. Both vessels took part in the Battle of Leyte Gulf and ended the war out of fuel and stranded near Kure, where they were attacked by Allied planes and sunk in the shallows; right: The breech of a sixteen-inch gun aboard the Japanese battleship *Nagato* in August 1945.

nearly thirty-three miles with great precision. They were the only guns of this calibre ever mounted in a ship. The three-gun turrets for these weapons weighed 2,774 tons each, and each armour-piercing projectile for the guns weighed half again as much as its counterpart for the sixteen-inch guns of *Iowa*, the ultimate American battleship class. And in creating these weapons for the *Yamato* class ships, Japan's naval weapons planners determined to produce the most powerful battleships in the world, battleships that even the industrial strength of the United States could not hope to equal.

When interviewed for a 1989 *New York Daily News* article, gunners serving in the USS *Wisconsin* spoke of the pride they felt in their jobs. Billy Owens of Corpus Christi, Texas: "This is a gunner's mate's ultimate dream—to be on the biggest guns, where you can climb right up through'em if you want. For us gunner's mates it doesn't seem noisy when they go off. To hear them go off, well, that's part of it. Little guns, you get a bang. This one, you get a boom." Gunner's Mate Chief Robert Durham of Deridder, Louisiana: "It's the lure of the battleship, the lure of the gunner's art. I feel that we're firing something that's a piece of history." And Gunner's Mate Chief Robert Loos of Youngstown, Ohio: "It's a rare assignment to come aboard a battleship at all. To be attached to the turret, well, that's the top of the list. I don't know anyone who wouldn't like the chance. It's just pure awesome power."

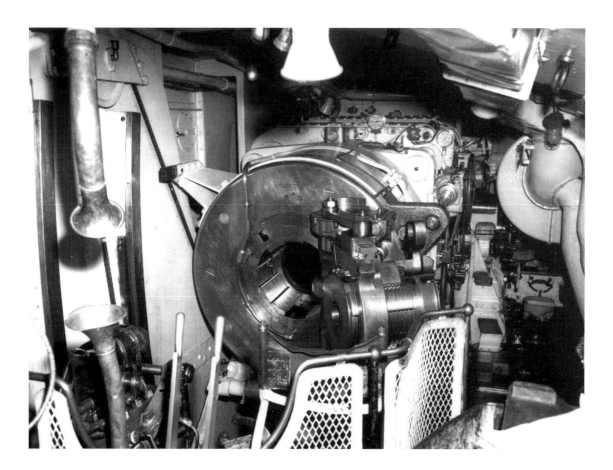

Bismarck

The German battleship
Bismarck at sea.

They were the biggest and most sophisticated battleships in the world when they were launched in early 1939. Adolf Hitler himself launched the 41,700-ton *Bismarck* at the Blohm und Voss Shipyard in Hamburg on 14 February, and her sister ship, *Tirpitz*, was launched at Wilhelmshaven in April. The great warships were a propaganda bonanza for Germany and the Nazis took full advantage of it. The Allies would not learn the actual dimensions and specifications of the *Bismarck* class battleships until after the end of World War Two.

These warships were planned expressly to attack and destroy the vital commerce of Germany's enemies on the Atlantic sea lanes. It was the intention of Admiral Erich Raeder, Commander-in-Chief of the German Navy, that *Bismarck* and *Tirpitz*, in company with the battlecruisers *Scharnhorst* and *Gneisenau*, should be sent into the Atlantic on their mission of disruption and destruction as soon as the big battleships had completed their sea trials in 1941. It was not to be. *Gneisenau* had sustained heavy damage while at St Nazaire when the Brittany port was bombed by the RAF in April, and *Scharnhorst* required a refit. *Tirpitz*, meanwhile, was still out conducting her trials. Only *Bismarck*, of the four vessels, was ready for action that spring.

Raeder then formed a new hunting battle group of *Bismarck* and the heavy cruiser *Prinz Eugen*, under the command of Vizeadmiral Günter Lütjens. Its task on deployment was to work together in attacks on enemy merchant shipping. *Bismarck* would attract the attentions of the British warships escorting the merchant vessels in convoy, while *Prinz Eugen* would attack the merchant ships. On 19 May, two heavily armed and armoured German warships

The launching of *Bismarck* in 1939, left, and below, her fitting-out.

sailed from the port of Götenhafen, heading west between Denmark and Sweden, around the south coast of Norway to Bergen. Their progress was recorded by an RAF Spitfire photo-reconnaissance plane and was reported to the Commanderin-Chief of the Royal Navy's Home Fleet at Scapa Flow, Admiral Sir John Tovey. In Scapa lay the proud new battleships *Prince of Wales* and *King George V*, as well as the new aircraft carrier *Victorious* and the battlecruiser *Hood*. Tovey dispatched *Prince of Wales* and *Hood* to Iceland on 21 May, where they were to guard that approach into the Atlantic. He had the heavy cruiser *Norfolk* on station in the Denmark Strait and she would soon be joined there by her sister ship, the *Suffolk*. Late that night, *Bismarck* and *Prinz Eugen* made their way out of Bergen to the open sea, turning northwest towards Iceland.

All day on the 22nd the weather in that part of the world deteriorated, making further photo-reconnaissance flights by the RAF impossible. Tovey got no additional reports on the movements of the German warships until late in the day when conditions improved and he learned that *Bismarck* and *Prinz Eugen* had left Norwegian waters. The next morning he left Scapa in his flagship, *King George V*, accompanied by the carrier *Victorious*, four cruisers and six destroyers.

The two German warships approached the northern edge of Iceland on 23 May and turned southwest into the Denmark Strait. The first sighting of *Bismarck* by a lookout on *Suffolk* came at 7:22 p.m. when the two ships were about seven miles apart. Patches of heavy mist and fog shrouded the area and *Suffolk* quickly entered the safety of one. She was soon

German Chancellor Adolf Hitler's only visit to the battleship *Bismarck*; page 120: A scene from the Twentieth Century Fox Film Corp. movie *Sink The Bismarck*.

joined by *Norfolk*, but not before the latter had been spotted by *Bismarck*, which fired several rounds at the cruiser. Sheltered in the mist, the two British warships settled in to keep track of their adversaries while Admiral Tovey's battle squadrons hurried to the scene. Vizeadmiral Lütjens was aware of the enemy cruisers, but not of Tovey's approaching vessels.

Prince of Wales and *Hood* were, at this point, approximately 500 miles due south and proceeding at high speed on course to intercept the *Bismarck* and *Prinz Eugen*, expecting to encounter them early in the morning of the 24th. Now the weather became worse, with snow and reduced visibility. The British cruisers lost contact with the German ships, but regained it just before 3 a.m.

Prince of Wales was a new 36,750-ton battleship which had been rushed into service before a proper period of sea trials could be carried out. Work on her main armament continued even as she steamed towards *Bismarck*. Her armour was far superior to that of *Hood*, with a fifteen-inch-thick armoured belt and five to six-inch deck plating. She mounted ten fourteen-inch guns.

The 41,200-ton battlecruiser *Hood* had been designed during World War One. She was old but powerfully armed with eight fifteen-inch guns, and was still fast and formidable. Her armour was suspect, however, being relatively thin on her afterdeck; a worrisome prospect against a ship like *Bismarck*, which was capable of lobbing her fifteen-inch shells at a high angle from a long range. Britain's largest battlecruiser, *Hood* had been an icon of British naval power for many years. In command of *Hood* and *Prince of Wales* was Vice Admiral Sir Lancelot Holland, on board *Hood*.

At 5:25 a.m. *Bismarck* and *Prinz Eugen* were sighted by the lookouts of *Prince of Wales*.

re steaming on a heading that allowed them to use
Bismarck was able to bring all of his main guns to
ice Admiral Holland had positioned his ships in this
m the plunging, long-range fire of *Bismarck*.

fire on the German ships at 5:52 a.m. He directed
enemy vessel, which he had mistakenly identified as
The Germans immediately returned fire, dropping
lls from *Bismarck* began to straddle *Hood*, and now
rated on *Hood*, sending a salvo into her which start-
as now directing all of her firing onto the *Bismarck*.
ps began adjusting their positions in order to bring
tly after 6 a.m., a new salvo from *Bismarck* found its
llen sky as the battlecruiser's aft ammunition maga-
stern. The great ship immediately listed to starboard
rself. Then she began leaning to port and continued
ees of list, she could not recover. In less than three
pping rapidly beneath the surface. From her entire

ugen now shifted their attention to *Prince of Wales*,
royed, killing all personnel there except Captain John
noperative and he discreetly chose to withdraw his
s decided against pursuing the wounded *Prince of*
t Nazaire for repairs to the damage she had incurred
cruisers *Norfolk* and *Suffolk* in shadowing *Bismarck*.
Prinz Eugen to continue out into the Atlantic on her

"Sink the Bismarck, at any cost," ordered Winston Churchill on 24 May when news of *Hood*"s loss reached the British people. With that, Admiral Tovey redirected vessels of the Home Fleet, including the 33,950-ton battleship *Rodney*, to the hunt for the German ship. *Rodney* mounted nine sixteen-inch guns and would ably complement Tovey's flagship, *King George V*, the battlecruiser *Repulse*, and the carrier *Victorious* in their pursuit of *Bismarck*. While rushing to intercept the German battleship, Tovey ordered several Swordfish and Fulmar aircraft from *Victorious* to mount a torpedo attack against *Bismarck*, but the results were negligible.

S70 2BR

A still from the Twentieth Century Fox Film Corp, movie *Sink The Bismarck* starring Kenneth More, Dana Wynter, and Carl Möhner.

Further stills from the 1960 Twentieth Century Fox Film Corp. movie, *Sink The Bismarck*, directed by Lewis Gilbert.

One of the last photos of the German battleship *Bismarck* before her sinking; right: The commander of the *Bismarck*, Vizeadmiral Johann Günther Lütjens.

Vizeadmiral Lütjens ordered a course change during the early morning hours of 25 May and soon managed to lose the shadowing *Norfolk*, *Suffolk* and *Prince of Wales*. Tovey, with no reliable information coming in on the whereabouts of *Bismarck*, guessed Lütjens' intentions. He turned his group of hunters northeast towards Iceland, while Lütjens continued to head southeast towards St Nazaire. It was early evening before Tovey knew he had guessed wrong and altered course again to the southeast. But Lütjens too, guessed wrong. He believed that the British were still tracking *Bismarck* on radar, when, in fact, they were not. He thought he had nothing to lose in sending a lengthy signal to his overseers in France, reporting that he was still being shadowed by three British warships, describing *Bismarck*'s action against the *Hood*, and giving his ship's present position, for which the British, who were intercepting the signal, were undoubtedly grateful.

The crew of an RAF Catalina flying boat piloted by U.S. Navy ensign Leonard Smith on a routine patrol, aided by Ultra intercepts from Bletchley Park in England, spotted *Bismarck* at 10:30 a.m. on 26 May and radioed her position to Admiral Tovey. The admiral's only real chance of catching the German battleship now lay with Force H, which was north of Gibraltar and heading towards *Bismarck*. Force H was composed of the aircraft carrier *Ark Royal*, the battlecruiser *Renown* and the cruiser *Sheffield*. *Sheffield* was the first to locate *Bismarck* and took up the job of shadowing her.

In the mid-afternoon, fourteen Swordfish torpedo bombers left *Ark Royal* to attack *Bismarck*, but mistakenly launched their torpedoes at *Sheffield*. Luckily for the British cruiser, the new-type fuses in the Swordfish torpedoes failed to function and *Sheffield* was unscathed. The Swordfish of *Ark Royal* tried again at just after 7 p.m. Fifteen of the biplanes that were

launched from the carrier, with old-style fuses in their weapons, reached *Bismarck* in two hours and began their attack. Two torpedoes struck the battleship, one hitting the armoured belt amidships and doing no significant damage. The other hit aft near the ship's rudders, jamming them. The pride of the German Navy was now unable to steer, a sitting duck. Her crew soon lost all hope of escaping the British pursuers. They were harassed through the night by five Royal Navy *Tribal* class destroyers which continued to attack *Bismarck* with torpedoes, though none of them hit their target.

King George V and *Rodney* steamed into view of the German battleship at first light on 27 May. The firing began at 8:47 a.m. *Rodney's* big guns fired first, but as soon as the distance between the two battleships had narrowed to less than twelve miles, they both opened fire. By *Bismarck's* third salvo, her gunners had straddled *Rodney*. It should have spelled the end for the British ship, but *Bismarck's* inability to manoeuvre had sealed her fate. In thirteen minutes, shells from the two British warships heavily damaged *Bismarck*, ruining Anton and Bruno, her forward turrets, her forecastle and her bridge. Though a flaming mess, she remained afloat but no longer able to fight from her main fire control station. Her remaining firing capability came from her after-director and that was soon put out of action. Over the next hour both *Rodney* and *Norfolk* continued their efforts to sink the sturdy *Bismarck*, now with torpedoes, but to no avail. Then, in mid-morning, the Royal Navy cruiser *Dorsetshire* moved into the area from the west where she had been escorting a convoy. At 10:25 a.m. she fired three torpedoes at *Bismarck*. The helpless battleship rolled in the waves, with much of her main deck awash. At 10:39 a.m. she rolled over and lay on her side. In seconds she went down and was gone. The largest, finest ship in the history of the German Navy sank on the ninth day of her maiden voyage. Of her crew of more than 2,200 men, just 115 survived, rescued by the *Dorsetshire*, the destroyer *Maori*, and the U-boat *U-74*.

"Thank you for showing me all of mankind's lofty ideals. Now let me introduce you to the basement."
—Sigmund Freud

"Don't cheer, boys, the poor devils are dying."
—Captain John Philip at the battle of Santiago, 1898

"A great Empire will be destroyed, an Empire which it was never my intention to destroy or even to harm . . . I consider myself in a position to make this appeal since I am not the vanquished begging favours, but the victor speaking in the name of reason."
—Adolf Hitler addressing the Reichstag, 19 July 1940

"Great as is our loss in the *Hood*, the *Bismarck* must be regarded as the most powerful, as she is the newest battleship in the world; and this striking of her from the German Navy is a very definite simplification of the task of maintaining the effective mastery of the northern seas and the maintenance of the northern blockade. I daresay that in a few days it will be possible to give a much more detailed account, but the essentials are before the House, and although there is shade as well as light in this picture, I feel that we have every reason to be satisfied with the outcome of this fierce and memorable naval encounter."
—Prime Minister Winston Churchill, from his speech to the House of Commons, 27 May 1941

Commander Alan Swanton, Fleet Air Arm, died aged 85 in January 2003. Swanton was one of the Swordfish pilots who attacked the German battleship *Bismarck* on 26 May 194, northeast of Brest. He had taken off from the carrier *Ark Royal* in appalling weather conditions, believing it to be the final air strike of the day. Initially, his squadron erroneously attacked the British cruiser *Sheffield*. After returning to the carrier to rearm and refuel, Swanton and fourteen other Swordfish pilots and crews took off again and most of them were immediately separated in the thick cloud. Swanton and his flight managed to keep together in the murk, located the *Bismarck* and attacked from her port side. Approaching through extremely accurate radar-controlled German flak, both Swanton and his air gunner were wounded, but he was able to continue the attack and get back to *Ark Royal* where he landed safely. There he learned that the squadron's torpedoes had jammed the rudders of the German battleship, crippling and leaving her a sitting duck in further British attacks.

right: Survivors of the *Bismarck*
being rescued by the crew of
the British heavy cruiser, HMS
Dorsetshire. on 27 May 1941.

below: Construction of the battleship *Tirpitz*, sister ship of the
Bismarck; bottom: The *Tirpitz* at sea;
bottom right: The demise of the
Tirpitz on 12 November 1944.

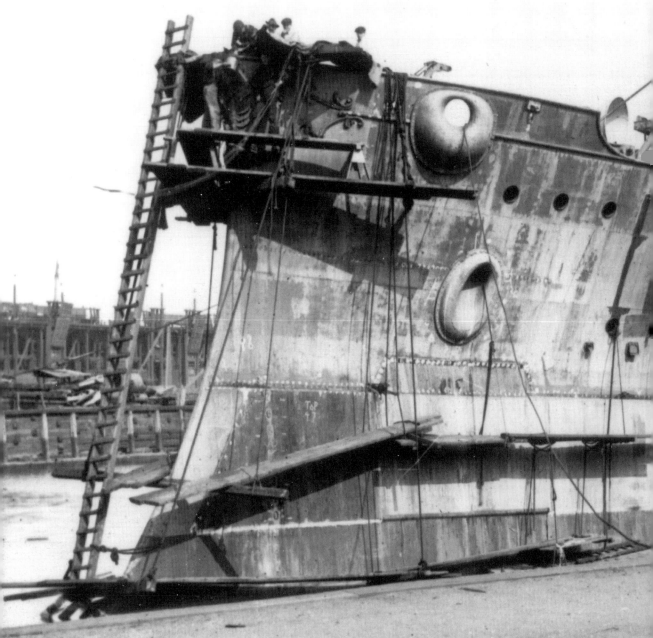

The USS *Idaho*, BB-24, was the second ship of the *Mississippi* class of U.S. Navy battleships. In 1914, she was transferred to the Greek Navy where she served for twenty-seven years. She was sunk by German aircraft in April 1941.

HMS *Vanguard* was a British fast battleship built during World War Two. She was the last battleship to be launched in the world.

When, after two atomic bombs were dropped on the Japanese cities of Hiroshima and Nagasaki in August of 1945, Japan finally surrendered to the Allies, ending World War Two, the formal surrender ceremonies were held aboard the battleship USS *Missouri* anchored in Tokyo Bay. Today the *Missouri* lies pierside at Ford Island in Pearl Harbor, a floating museum and popular tourist attraction. The *Missouri* was the last battleship built by the United States.

U.S.S. MISSOURI

OVER THIS SPOT
ON 2 SEPTEMBER 1945
THE INSTRUMENT
OF FORMAL SURRENDER
OF JAPAN TO THE ALLIED POWERS
WAS SIGNED
THUS BRINGING TO A CLOSE
THE SECOND WORLD WAR

THE SHIP AT THAT TIME
WAS AT ANCHOR
IN TOKYO BAY

LATITUDE 35° 21' 17" NORTH ∼ LONGITUDE 139° 45' 36" EAST

above right: The USS *Iowa* entering Pearl Harbor. The Iowa class battleships were like fully-equipped small cities in their facilities. In their later years they were also equipped with cruise missiles and drone aircraft; below: The place on the starboard side of the hull where a Japanese kamikaze aircraft impacted late in World War Two; below right: A still from the Warner Bros. battleship movie *Under Siege*, with Steven Seagal, Tommy Lee Jones and Gary Busey; far right: A chow line in the *Missouri*, now a museum in Pearl Harbor, Hawaii.

top left: The USS *Mississippi*; above: HMS *Dreadnought*; left: USS *North Dakota*; below: USS *Texas*; bottom left and right: USS *Alabama* under construction; right: The USS *Iowa*, USS *Colorado*, and USS *West Virginia* gathered in Japan in October 1945.

U.S.S. ALABAMA (BB60)

The USS *Louisiana*, BB-19, an American contemporary of HMS *Dreadnought*, in April 1908 near Coronado, California.

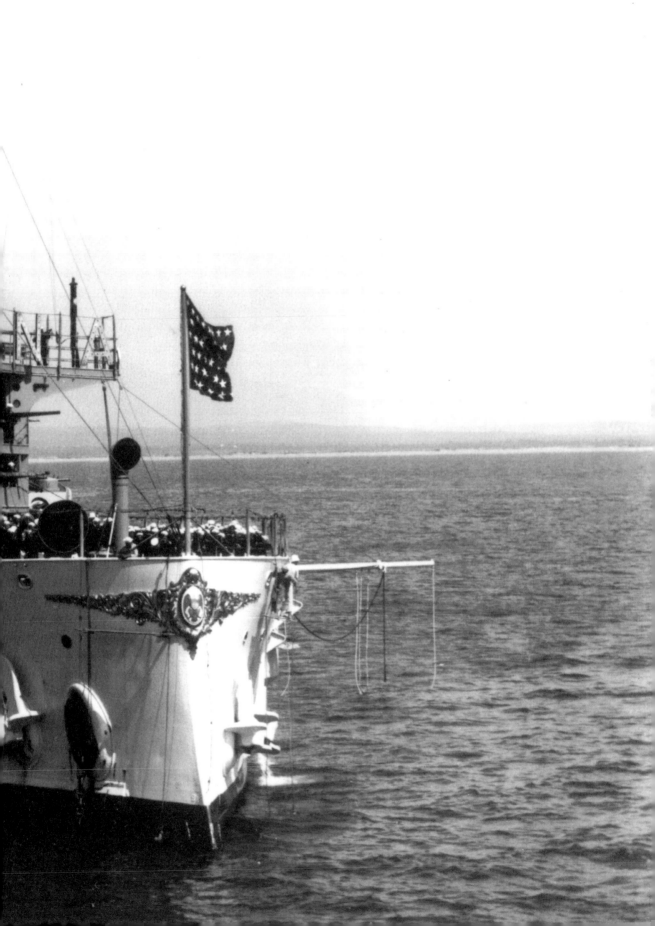

Grateful acknowledgment is made to the following for the use of their previously published material: Coward, B.R., RN, for extracts from his book *Battleship At War*, Ian Allan, 1987; Ebert, Roger, for an extract from his column on *The Battleship Potemkin*; Gilbey, Joseph, for extracts from his book *Langsdorff of the Graf Spee, Prince of Honour*; HMS *Victory* website for extracts; Kipling, Rudyard, for extracts from his book *Sea Warfare*, Macmillan and Co., 1916; Manchester, William, for an extract from his book *Goodbye Darkness*, Little Brown, 1980; Mason, Ted, for extracts from his book *Battleship Sailor*, Naval Institute Press, 1982; Mitsuro, Yoshida, for extracts from his book *Requiem for Battleship Yamato*, University of Washington Press, 1999; Wouk, Herman, for an extract from his book *The Caine Mutiny*, Jonathan Cape Ltd., 1951; Royal Navy, for extracts from the booklet *Your Ship, Notes and Advice To An Officer On Assuming His First Command*.

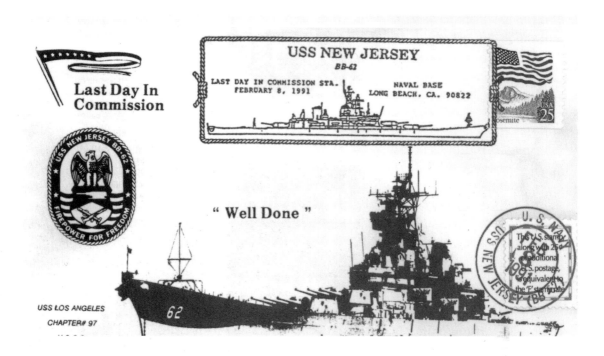